CW00553583

How to Find Yourself:

Explore your Personality, Self-Discovery, Self-Awareness, and Life Design for Maximum Fulfillment

by Nick Trenton
www.NickTrenton.com

Table of Contents

Introduction

It's a tale as old as time: someone reaches middle age and suddenly, they're in "crisis." They seem to wake up one morning and look at everything with fresh eyes. It's as though the party's over and the lights in the club have been turned on, and they're seeing everything and everyone around them in a whole new (frightening) light.

A question forms in their minds: who am I, really?

They notice with alarm that the question is hard to answer. They also notice a creeping sense of dread; a feeling that they feel utterly lost where they are. All at once, they feel rudderless—what are they really doing in life, and what is it that they actually want? Nothing can be as disorienting as realizing that . . . you don't really know.

The Oracle at Delphi famously had the words inscribed with, "Know thyself."

It sounds nice, but if you've picked up this book, chances are you have no idea what knowing yourself actually looks like, or how to do it. There comes a point in many people's lives when they feel quite keenly that they have absolutely no idea who they are. Whether the sensation creeps up on them slowly, or it comes all at once after a major life event, it feels the same: like you're completely adrift in life and cannot begin to answer the question, "Who am I? And what do I really want out of this life?"

These can be heavy questions, no doubt. Before we start this book, however, there's one thing you should know: questioning who you are is one hundred percent normal. Seriously. Though it can feel like a major crisis to suddenly feel like a stranger to yourself, realize that confusion on this question is a completely human response to living in a frankly crazy world! If you're disoriented, overwhelmed, disappointed, exhausted, or just plain old confused—well, congratulations! These are the natural starting points for one of life's greatest challenges: discovering yourself.

This book is for you if:

- You feel inauthentic somehow, as though you're not really living the life you're meant to be
- You feel as though you've just been carried along with life, and haven't really *chosen* any particular path over another
- You feel uninspired, unfocused, and have a vague sense of not fulfilling your potential
- You don't know what you want
- You have trouble committing to an occupation, a relationship, or even a particular opinion or worldview
- You feel unsettled and unsure of yourself, as though you don't know what the purpose or meaning of your life really is
- You feel bored and as though you've lost all spark and zest for life
- You have trouble clearly identifying your strengths and weaknesses, and

don't have a strong sense of your
unique personality or path in life

If all this sounds familiar, you might be in
need of some good old fashioned soul-
searching—and that's where this book
comes in. Before we can answer the
question of who we are, though, we need to
be honest about *why* we're having so much
difficulty with the question in the first
place. If there are few things in life as
important as a solid understanding of
yourself as a person, then why is it
seemingly so difficult to figure it all out?

Why You're Having Trouble Knowing Who You Are

Though it seems like self-knowledge is
some arduous and long-winded journey, the
truth is that it's a normal and healthy state
of mind to know yourself and be in full
alignment with your purpose, your
interests, your strengths, and your
limitations. This bears repeating: self-
knowledge is a normal, natural state. The
problem is that we live in a world set up to

obscure this natural relationship we have with ourselves. Though we might come into the world complete and with a strong sense of what we want (have you ever seen a baby struggle to know what they want out of life?), we can soon lose sight of our own internal compass.

The Effect of Our Formative Years

When you grew up, you didn't just grow physically—you also grew your personality, preferences, memories, habits, beliefs (including the untrue and limiting ones), and your understanding of what was possible for yourself in the world. This happened in the backdrop of your family life. If your family was dysfunctional, you might have established a foundation for your sense of self that was less than stable. Our parents, siblings, and caregivers can teach us early on who we are, and at that young age, we absorb these narratives without question.

What did your family teach you about yourself?

Some of us barely think to ask the question because we so completely accept the identity we've been given. Maybe you're someone who was taught that your value as a person came down to how useful you were to others. Early on, maybe your parents installed this belief in you by praising and acknowledging you only when you helped others. You might have grown up with the unconscious beliefs, "I am good when other people think I'm good. I get what I need by helping other people with their needs," and so on.

Such a person may grow up to be a people-pleaser. Others might describe them in amazing terms, but when this person is alone with themselves, they may feel profoundly empty. What do *they* want? They're not even sure. Because they have spent so much time focusing their energy and attention externally, they are completely unused to looking inside themselves. They have only practiced serving the needs of others, and they have no idea what their own needs are.

This is the person who reaches midlife and feels burnt out and uninspired. They don't enjoy anything—it all feels like an obligation to them. They want to learn more about who they are, but they seek it externally. They ask their family to validate them. They go to a therapist and ask unconsciously, "Can you please tell me who I am?"

Maybe you came from a family where the unspoken lesson was, "Being different is bad." You learned that to get affection and care, you needed to obey and be like everyone else. Being raised this way, you might even feel like the path of personal discovery is just a selfish indulgence, or dangerous somehow, because you might find yourself abandoned or kicked out of "the group" if you try to be unique.

Without delving too deeply into it all just yet, can you start asking in a general way what your family taught you about your identity? What role did you play in the family? And how do you think these early experiences have shaped who you are now?

The Effect of Low Self-Esteem

A major roadblock on the way to learning more about who you truly are is the pre-existing belief that *you are bad*. This belief can be so deeply buried in our unconscious mind that we seldom even notice it anymore, but it's there anyway. Affecting everything, this feeling that we are somehow wrong or broken or bad or unlovable when compared to everyone else.

Many people are carrying around an enormous sense of shame that gets in the way of their self-knowledge. How *worthy* do you think you are as a human being right now? This can be a hard question to answer. But in answering it, you see the problem: why bother to learn more about someone who is completely worthless? Would you go on a journey to a place you already knew was boring and not worth visiting? Nope!

A great impediment to understanding ourselves better is the belief that, on a core level, we're not really worth getting to know better in the first place. Self-knowledge is an act that intrinsically assumes we count and we matter as people. Maybe you look at the prospect of self-love and think it's great . . . but for other people, not you. Self-discovery can't happen unless we think that our identity is something valuable and worth not only investigating, but caring for and cherishing.

The Effect of the Media

Let's come straight out and say it: advertising, media, and news are not interested in helping you find your truest and most authentic self. Their goal is to sway your opinion, to convince you of a story, or, most commonly, to get you to buy something. The best way to get someone to buy something? Draw their attention to all the ways that they are currently lacking and need the thing you're selling them. Make them keenly feel that something is missing in their lives—and for a price, you have that missing thing.

Media of all kinds works constantly to send you the message: you are incomplete. You need something else. If you have that already, then you need more of it. Something is lacking. *You* are lacking. After all, a completely satisfied and healthy individual is not easily manipulated into buying things they don't need. The trick is that all of these messages are usually hidden from you. You may be inspired to act and think that you chose to do so independently, because you genuinely wanted to be wealthier, more attractive, or have a cleaner bathroom than your neighbor does.

But all the while the message is still being felt: you're not enough just as you are. So you march onward with the mission to solve a problem that was entirely manufactured in the first place. You feel incomplete, unworthy, dissatisfied.

The next time you read the news or scroll through social media or watch a TV ad or flip through a magazine, ask yourself what core beliefs are being reinforced, and why. Notice how you feel. If you're feeling lost, a little pessimistic, and unsure who you are and what you want, you can rest assured that at least some of that feeling has been introduced to you by the media. It sounds sinister, but it's true: the ideal customer, reader, app-user (or even voter) is one who feels bad about themselves, and who doesn't really know what they want. Why? Because these are the people who can be *told* what they want.

The Effect of an Environment that Reinforces a Lack of Authenticity

If you're unsure of who you are on a deep level, if you feel bad about yourself or if you're stuck playing a role others have assigned you, you might find yourself in the company of other people who are living similarly inauthentic lives. When you wear a mask, you might find yourself surrounded by others who are also wearing masks.

You might have a mask—let's call it your ego or an identity you're very attached to—that has a particular impact on those around you. They respond to you and the mask, and in that way reinforce it. Your family may treat you a certain way when you adopt a certain attitude with them. Life itself may seem to reward certain behaviors and discourage others. Maybe you're in a workplace where vulnerability is treated as suspicious and dangerous, and where fake, insincere people are rewarded.

Where personal development is concerned, this point can be particularly painful: as we grow and find out who we are, we may discover that those around us actually don't like it. We may discover that our friends, family, and partners are attached to a vision of who we are that is not accurate or healthy, and if we change, we do risk causing disruption. In this way, our social environment can powerfully lock us into a way of being that doesn't feel like it's genuine.

You've probably heard of people who make massive life improvements only to find that the people they thought of as their friends actually preferred it when that person has low self-esteem and didn't achieve much. When one person removes a mask, it highlights that everyone else is wearing one and not removing theirs, and this can be very uncomfortable for everyone involved. Many people put off the dream of delving more deeply into who they are because, on some level, they know that doing so will completely turn their world upside down.

The Effect of Everyday Lifestyle Habits

The previous points have seemed rather enormous in scale—your upbringing, your culture, and so on. But we can also constantly create a life of authenticity for ourselves in the smaller, more everyday habits we choose. You see, the little things add up. In a real way, we are nothing more than the sum of all the tiny actions we take day in and day out. The small choices. Is your life cluttered with meaningless actions that undermine who you really are? Are you quietly opting for a phony life in little ways without realizing it?

Brick by brick, we can build a prison around ourselves with our lifestyle habits and our choices. Imagine someone who everyday fritters away money on purchases for a lifestyle they don't really have. Maybe they're pressured by others to buy certain things to keep up, as many people are in certain careers. Bit by bit, purchase by purchase, this person creates a life for themselves that is completely phony. They may one day look at it all (the wardrobe, the car, the gadgets, all of it) and feel completely alienated from it. Rather than feel at home in their lives, they look at their lives from afar, unable to identify with any of it. They are imposters in their own identity.

The Real Self and the False Self

As you can see above, there *is* an identity, only it's a false one. If a person struggling with their identity were to express their unease, people in their lives might say in confusion, "But what are you talking about? You already have an identity—you're a father/lawyer/American/golfer."

But we feel deep down that this ego, this collection of narratives, this story of the roles we've been assigned is **not** who we are. It is an identity, but it is not really ours, not authentic, not genuine. Something inside us tells us that there is something else, something more real, and we'd like to know it. We'd like to find our true identity amid all the noise and confusion. Sadly, finding out who we really are may feel isolating and uncomfortable, since we abandon the old identity that may have been a comfort. Whether you call it your soul, your genuine personality, your identity, or something else, this "real self" is what we're after. Without it, we can feel disconnected, aimless, depressed, and lonely. We might feel like we go through life in a fog.

Now, this isn't to say that social roles or people's expectations of us have no place in our identity. This isn't to say that our family histories or cultures don't or shouldn't have any bearing on who we are. Rather, it's about *consciously* being aware of what is a mask and what is real. It's about choosing to connect with our real selves and foregoing things that feel false, insincere, or pointless. When we do this, we are not only crystal clear about who we are, but we are *energized*—suddenly, the path forward seems illuminated, and we take joy in life again.

Take heart: your true self never went anywhere. It's still there! Our quest is just to find it again and reconnect to it—or connect to it for the first time. In the remainder of this book, we're going to dig more deeply into this thing called personality so that we have a language to talk about the things we discover about ourselves. We'll look at psychological models and theories of the self as a kind of road map for understanding our own inner terrains.

We'll also look at the role of the unconscious mind in shaping the false self, and how, when we become aware of these processes, we can start to take charge and become more fully who we actually are. By looking at attachment theory and the ideas around birth order, we can start to see in detail the effect our early childhood experiences have had on us. And finally, we'll look at Jung's psychological theories of self and see if they can help us gain a keener insight into the narratives we weave about our own identities.

At all times, we are not just looking at dry psychological theory for the fun of it. We are not intending to categorize ourselves (or others) neatly into boxes and call it a day. Rather, these are just tools that can help you get closer to the true self that already exists within you. In learning the vocabulary of personality psychology, you can equip yourself with the models and theories that allow you to become better acquainted with your genuine self.

The Benefits of Self-Knowledge

You might already be convinced of the value of self-discovery, and are rearing to go with the rest of the book. But if you're still ambivalent about whether self-knowledge is really a worthwhile goal, consider what is really at stake. For people habitually used to putting their own needs and well-being last, self-knowledge can feel like a wasteful indulgence, or a distraction from the stuff that really matters. But knowing who we are deep down is not frivolous—it could affect literally every area of your life—and the lives of those around you.

When you know yourself, you're happier. Plain and simple. This is because you don't spend effort and time on avoiding or denying who you are. You can relax and be open. When you can express who you are and what you want, other people can see you, and you are more likely to actually get the things you most need. You can let go of dull feelings of alienation and actually start to enjoy yourself—enjoy *your self.* You can gain immense satisfaction out of just being you. How great is that?

When you know yourself, you are not a divided or conflicted person. There are no secrets or masks or hidden agendas or unacknowledged dreams. You are not a mystery to others, and you don't have two faces. Everything—your words, actions, attitudes—are aligned in the same direction. You are at ease, and other people perceive that ease in you. Strangely, when you are behaving in congruence with your inner self, you are perceived as more honest and genuine, and this can elicit from others the same kind of honesty and openness. This can indirectly improve your connection to others.

When you know yourself, you act with clarity. Your choices are not made at random or because of pressure from the outside world. You do what you do because you choose it consciously, and because it fits in with who you are and what you want. You procrastinate less, you are more efficient, and you don't waste time on projects that don't matter to you. You seldom feel confused or unsure about the right way to behave or which path to take— knowing who you are answers all of this easily so you can just get on with it.

When you know yourself, you can better self-regulate. If you have a good understanding of your weaknesses, temptations, flaws, and blindspots, then you can take smart action to counter them. We can only improve those things that we are honest and conscious enough to admit are flaws in the first place. Thus, self-knowledge improves our willpower and determination. It gives us control over our weak points instead of us being controlled by them.

When you know yourself, you are immune to social pressure. That way that advertising and media gets in your head? You'll be more resistant to it. When people press on your boundaries or try to tell you who you are for their own benefit, you can see it and push against it. This allows you to develop deep, real confidence and determination in your destiny and your choices. You are not guilted into acting against your values, you are less easy to bully or manipulate, and you may even find yourself inspiring and leading others because you show the courage to be authentic with yourself.

When you know yourself, it's easier to have compassion for others. If you can look within and forgive the weak spots, and care for the worthwhile human being that you are, you learn to offer the same generosity and empathy to others. When you are confident in your unique self, you suddenly don't feel compelled to judge others for who they are. This, again, improves your relationships.

When you know yourself, life is just a lot more fun! All of the above makes it seem like self-knowledge is a very serious endeavor—nothing could be further from the truth. Truly understanding who you are is a bit like falling in love, or learning about an amazing new culture when traveling. The world seems so interesting, you feel inspired and excited, and life is filled with juiciness and novelty and possibility. There's no doubt about it: having a thorough idea of who you are means you live a richer, more meaningful, and more colorful life.

Chapter 1: Finding Your Values

If you've found yourself asking the question "who am I?", you might have also been asking simultaneously, "What should I do?"

Our lack of genuine identity can show itself in an inability to make decisions, to choose a path, to set a goal, or to say what we want—in other words, what we *do* is a reflection of who we *are*. If we have a problem with one, we usually have a problem with the other.

So, this is where we'll begin. If you're unsure of how to act, you're also probably a little unsure of who you are. Knowing how best to act is a question of knowing what kind of person you are. If you are someone who prioritizes family and social connection above anything else, for example, you don't need to think too hard about the dilemma of working late nights at the office versus spending quality time with your young children. Your identity informs your choices.

In fact, how we respond to life's dilemmas, choices, and difficulties says a lot about the strength of our own values. We are as we do, and we do according to what we value. Inner values and principles are like a personal manifesto that tells us how to act in any situation. This is our own code of ethics that we've devised for ourselves, and it acts like a guiding light even when—or maybe particularly when—the path is unclear.

How shall we define "values"?

A value is a judgment that makes claims about the priorities we hold in life. **They are principles, rules, or beliefs that give meaning to our lives.** They are what stop life from feeling empty and meaningless, because they are inherently *about* meaning—it's whenever you say, "Thing A is more important and valuable than thing B." In saying this, it follows that the right thing to do is thing A.

Values not only guide our action when we're unclear, they give us strength to carry on when the path might be clear but the journey difficult. You might have a really difficult time turning down those extra hours at work, but when you can tune into the deeper value of being present in your children's lives as they grow up, you are given strength to make a decision that makes you unpopular at work.

Granted, many of the values you might hold, consciously or unconsciously, are secondhand. They come to us from our cultures, our parents, our religion, our political environment, even our historical era. Some values might be held uncritically, i.e. you may have them simply out of habit, and haven't really examined them closely. Others might be personally chosen after extensive deliberation. Values can change over time. We might rebel against the values of our group, accept them completely, or negotiate a little, but we always have the option to be more conscious and deliberate about our own values. If you were put on the spot right now and asked what your values were, how quickly and easily do you think you could answer? Do you think you could easily list five or ten of the things you most value in life? Going even further, could you say confidently that your life mostly aligns with these values? It's one thing to *know* what's right, but there's very little point in devising a complete book of rules that you never really intend to follow.

Don't Choose Your Core Values, Clarify Them

Though the self-help industry might sometimes have you believe otherwise, your identity isn't just something you go shopping for like you do a pair of sneakers or a brand of shampoo. You cannot just pick and choose values—they need to be a *genuine* expression of what you really do care about. This can seem a little like a catch-22 situation—you don't have an identity so you need to find your values, but how do you know which values you care about without having an identity?

The process is not as difficult as it seems.

Firstly, know that the process isn't done all at once—you are not going to uncover a complete and fully-functioning self in an afternoon and start living your best life once you wake up tomorrow morning. It's a *process*, and insight will come in fits and starts. In fact, a life well-loved might be one in which you continually revisit the question of identity, with your answers deepening on every attempt.

We also need to remember that, in finding values, we are the ultimate arbiters. We decide. So, you might need to take the time to tune out every other voice so you can better hear your own. There is no wrong way to do it. There's no right answer. There's only what works for *you*.

Having said that, people are motivated by a lot of different values, which it might help to consider in finding out our own:

Financial independence or wealth

Being in nature

Romantic love or connection with others

Having freedom and independence

Learning and knowledge

Fun and adventure

Good physical health and fitness

Spiritual or religious pursuits

Art and creativity

Work accomplishments, leadership, business

Security and survival

Social cohesion and harmony in a group

Peace, calm, and contentment; relaxation

Honor, loyalty, and dependability

. . . and so on.

You might look at all of the above and think that they're all valuable. But the trick is in identifying your *priorities*—those things that are best, that bring the most satisfaction and meaning. You may care about creative expression and individuality, but your love of family stability may trump that ten times over. You need to know how each of your needs and preferences rank relative to each another.

A good way to find out what matters most is to ask what has seemingly bought you the most happiness and sense of meaning in the past. If you look at all your high points in life, and they all involved adventure and freedom to travel and explore, that tells you something. It works the other way around too: in thinking of your life's most painful memories, why did they hurt so much? Could it be that these events were moments when your deepest values were disappointed or violated? Tally up the achievements you're genuinely proud of and see what they have in common. Or, look more closely at your worst failures and blunders and ask why they stung particularly badly—were these times where you acted *against* your values?

Another trick is to look at the people you admire or wish to be like (or even envy)—what values do they exemplify? If all your role models and heroes are self-made entrepreneurs, is this telling you about the value you place on financial independence? Maybe. Or maybe what appeals to you about them is that they're unique and following their own dreams, breaking the rules. Or maybe they are reflecting your yearning for a life filled with more admiration and recognition.

Since you are uncovering your values rather than creating them from scratch, another general technique is to look at all the decisions you are currently making—they may speak strongly to values you might not yet be aware you actually have. Watch yourself closely for a few days or a week, and notice your decisions when faced with a choice to make. Notice how you feel when you choose one thing over another.

It might be that you notice yourself often choosing things that leave you feeling bad, and don't really feel aligned with who you are. It may be that you notice key decisions reflecting your values. Either way, we are already living by values every moment of every day—it's simply a question of becoming aware of them and asking whether they're the choices that best reflect the values we hold—or want to hold.

Look for patterns. See if you can find any strong feelings one way or another—are there any non-negotiable sentiments? What are you absolutely unwilling to do or give up? Why? What choices make you feel proud and content, and which ones feel like a compromise, an obligation, or even something you're embarrassed about?

Feeling right, however, is just one aspect that helps determine your values. You also need to make informed decisions about what you really believe in that rely on more than just your emotional inclinations at any given time. Say you're confused about whether you value your career or your connection with friends and family more. You've found that abandoning your family for work often leaves you feeling guilty, and so you think maybe you value your family more than your career. The next step here is to try to find out *why* you feel that way. There can be many factors external to yourself that are influencing this feeling of guilt. Maybe you just have FOMO (fear of missing out), or your family has ingrained a value system in you that says work should always come second.

To get a clearer picture of what valuing something really entails, it helps to read a little on the various reasons why one might want to prioritize something over the other. We are rarely aware of all the reasons one or the other might be a good idea. Just a few searches will yield several reasons for either choice. When reading these, don't just think about which reasons sound more appealing, think about what feels *right* to you. These will often have a lot to do with what your goals in life are. Are you really ready to sacrifice personal success to have a stronger bond with your family? Or would you rather focus on your career while ensuring your family is important, but not paramount? Thinking in this way will prevent you from repeating the earlier cycle of simply having imbibed certain values from your surroundings without really considering what matters most to *you*.

Values (and the identity that comes with them) are not abstract. They are real, lived things, out there in the world. They express themselves in actions and choices. True, they may not always be expressed perfectly all the time. But the *intention* is to live by them. They are a yardstick by which to measure your life, whether you achieve that standard or not. This is why it's more effective to look at your actual life in action when considering values, rather than just sitting down with a piece of paper and pulling nice-sounding ideas out of your imagination. Remember, we are striving for the *real* self, and not just another false self.

What About My Goals?

Be honest with yourself. **In asking what you value, you are halfway on the road to knowing who you are, and when you know who you are, you know how to act, and why**. In trying to find your identity, you might be tempted to start thinking about your goals in life. But this is premature. You can only decide on your goals when you know what you value (and don't value!). How many of us have chosen a goal, only to reach it and realize it isn't what we really wanted, or it doesn't have the desired effect on us? It's probably because we didn't stop to think whether our goals actually lined up with our values.

Goals are important, but they emerge from our values—not the other way around. Yes, your interests and preferences matter. Your obligations and commitments matter. You need to make plans and understand your strengths and weaknesses. But all of this comes after you do the important work of setting up your values. Without them, you cannot undertake any other task with clarity, and you will have that nagging sense of aimlessness in your life—no matter how many impressive-sounding goals you come up with.

When we have our values clearly identified within us, it's as though life is suddenly clearly outlined, and we can see what is inside that outline and what is outside. We know what is relevant to us, and what is a distraction or a diversion. We know how to assess things, and how to measure our actions. We know where we're going and what we stand for. And all of this adds up to a life that feels *purposeful*. We don't feel wishy-washy or unsure of ourselves— instead, our identify firmly takes shape, and we are consciously aware of who we are and what we're doing. It's very simple: we cannot be fulfilled if we don't have values. Without values, we have nothing to compare our achievements against, and all our actions feel pointless. With values, however, life just flows so much more smoothly.

Consider an example. Someone might work hard to discover that their primary value in life is spiritual enrichment. Looking at their lives, they see how so much of their joy has come from reading spiritual and religious texts, volunteering, going to retreats, meditating, and taking plenty of time to be in nature, where they feel closest to the divine.

Because this value is strongly identified, it acts as a guiding force for everything in this person's life. When they're feeling depressed, they know to stop and ask, "Am I neglecting my spiritual needs? How can I reconnect to that feeling that sustains me and gives me hope?" When faced with a conflict with themselves or with others, they fall back on their code of ethics that comes from their values—they approach problems with compassion, forgiveness, and a little humor.

When they're standing in the checkout line at the supermarket and they see a trashy tabloid paper with a cover designed to inflame and aggravate, this person is able to stop, take a breath, and say, is this me? Is that who I want to be? Then they can turn away and choose not to engage with that kind of material in their life. What you eat and drink, what you say, where you live, the work you do, the clothes you wear—all of this reflects who you are and what you value. In this way, both big and small value decisions create a framework and a foundation for an entire life. When clarified this way, you can see how powerful it is to know one's own values.

Here's the thing: you already have values. Whether you got them from your family, your society, or Instagram, you have them. Whether you're aware of them or not, they're there, guiding your life. So why not make sure the values you have are something you consciously want?

We need to be careful that we are always tuning in to the *real self*, and not another *false self*. How many times have we heard about the person having a midlife crisis, or a teenager going through "a phase"? They seem to be trying on a few costumes in the attempt to settle on one that fits. People in these transitional states of life may cling to an identity they think they *should* have, or wished they did have, but it is still not a genuine reflection of who they are. This work takes patience, honesty, and a little determination (and yes, you may need to go through a few awkward "phases" yourself on the way!).

Now that we've seen what value-discovery *isn't* (it's not about goals, other people's opinions, or switching out one false self for another one), we can look more closely at what it is. Here's a step-by-step guide to bring you closer.

Value Clarification, Step by Step

STEP ONE: CLEAR YOUR MIND

If we wish to fill ourselves up with something new, we first need to pour out all the old that's already there, and start fresh. We need to let go of any bias, expectations, or preconceived notions. Being fixed in our thinking, we can imagine we already know the answer to everything—but this understandably undermines the process of discovery. You really need to trust that there is something for you to learn, something unknown out there that you are willing to encounter openly.

It's difficult, but try to drop (at least temporarily) any preconceived ideas about who you are. Your conscious mind may want to jump in and tell you a narrative ("you're an introvert, you're a worrier, you're XYZ"), but set these aside and give some space for your unconscious mind to come to the fore and see new possibilities. We have all been taught which values are "better" than others—we need to forget this lesson if we want to find our *own* values for ourselves!

STEP TWO: START A LIST

Remember that values aren't chosen, they're clarified. Trust that you already have them, you just have to *discover* them. You don't want to inadvertently write down a list of all the things that other people expect you to be.

Scan the list given earlier and see if any of them spark your interest. If not quite, how could you tweak them so they seem more valuable in your opinion? When compiling a list, start broadly and don't censor yourself. Add anything that strikes you as important. You might begin by writing "love," but on further reflection, tease that out a bit more. What kind of love, and why? You might decide that what you really value is brotherly love, friendships, belonging to a community. You could then put "community" on the list and see if that spurs any further values.

As you go, draw on both your best and worst life memories to guide you, as described above. The moments you felt most yourself—what was happening, and what were you doing? The moments when you felt frustrated, violated, disappointed, or uncomfortable—what was not happening, and what does this tell you about the feelings you hold dear?

You might recall the greatest day of your life so far, the birth of your first child. In thinking about why this felt so amazing, you jot a few more notes on your list. You realize that you felt a deep, deep sense of purpose knowing that you now had someone to look after. You examine those feelings of hope, of dedication, of amazement. You realize that being a parent satisfies some of your core values—selfless love, belonging, trust, and hope for the future.

Ask yourself questions to dig closer toward those things in life that bring a sense of meaning. What makes a good day good? What makes you proud and grateful? What makes life worth living (i.e. you'd be miserable without it)? Look not only at the standards you hold for yourself, but those you hold for others. What is a deal breaker for you in your relationships? What is your idea of a person *not* living a meaningful and purposeful life?

STEP THREE: PULL IT ALL TOGETHER

Eventually, you should have a long list of things you value. Though all of these things are important, they can probably be distilled down to a few *main* core values. Read over the notes you've made and see if you can group them into chunks. For example, "community," "friendship," and "compassion for others" have a lot in common, as do "independence," "freedom to follow my own path," and "part-time employment."

Remember, you are not judging anything you have on the list. If you genuinely identify it as a value, put it down. If, on further reflection, you really don't care all that much about innovation or winning awards, then leave them out. As you work (without attachment or judgment!), you should start seeing some clarity emerge. As much as you can, try to connect these ideas to real life—are these values you've actually experienced before meaningful, or have you just been raised or socialized to assume that you want them?

Once you have some clusters of values, see if you can dig deep and identify the main theme uniting them all. In our examples above, friendship, compassion, and community all have one thing in common: the joy of shared human connection. Take your time with this—what is it, really, that makes all of the things on your list so appealing to you?

STEP FOUR: RANK YOUR VALUES

Some people might find that, even after clustering, they're still left with a big list. But, life is filled with choices, and since we are limited, we are often called on to choose between two important and worthwhile things. This is why we need to clarify further and prioritize our values.

You now want to whittle down to those essential values that you absolutely cannot live without. The most fundamental, most basic needs of yours, without which you'd be completely lost, miserable, or pointless. Even if you can identify a few of these, try to choose between five and ten values that you feel neatly capture the dimensions of what's most important to you.

Then, rank them in order of importance. You might do this in ten minutes or find you need a few days to really contemplate it deeply. Use your feelings as a guide, and remember not to rush—you are setting aside everything you know about your false self so that you can meet the acquaintance of your real self—that takes time!

STEP FIVE: LET YOUR VALUES COME ALIVE

If you write something like "physical health and fitness" as a core value, it may seem a little abstract. Time to embed this sentiment out in the real world and put it into context! You want to put these newly discovered core values into a shorthand form that will inspire you every time you look at it, and remind you precisely of the best things in life—according to your most authentic self.

For the person valuing physical fitness, a single beautiful image of a ballet dancer in a powerful leaping pose, mid-flight, might capture the essence of what you value so much: pushing against the limits of human physicality to find beauty and expression in the joy of having a living, moving body. Or, you might find that a certain phrase or quote captures your core value better, a bit like a mission statement. Find a stimulus that triggers a strong emotional reaction— it's these emotions that point you in the right direction and speak more directly to your inner self than any dry, abstract language could.

STEP SIX: TRY THEM ON FOR SIZE

No, you're not done quite yet! Value discovery is an ongoing process. Once you've identified and condensed your core values, see how they fit out in real life. Leave the list for a while and come back to it, seeing how it feels. Do you feel comfortable, in alignment, and clear . . . or are some things still not quite feeling like "you"? Look for the hidden voice of your parents, your culture, etc., and ask whether they've been swaying your list or the way you rank things. If your intuition pipes up, listen to what it says. This may sometimes feel like vague, flimsy work, but rest assured that you are exploring exciting new realms that many people never give themselves permission to enter.

And that's that. Your core values distilled into a concentrated essence that tells you a lot about who you are as a person, and helps you answer a range of questions from, "What should I do?" to, "What do I want right now?"

Putting Your Values to Work

Of course, values aren't just things you "have." Discovering your values is about so much more than simply creating a list. **Your identity is what results when you express your values in the world**. In other words, a consistently lived value becomes identity.

Once you have comfortably identified a core value list that makes you happy, you need to do the hard work of asking how well you actually manifest this value in your own life. Many people claim that they value their families and children more than anything, but anyone could look at their life and see that on the ground, that person doesn't spend any time at home, forgets their kids' birthdays, and just recently spent their college money on a sports car.

That person may truly value their family, but their actions are badly out of alignment with that value. It's time for you to see how much these values are actually appearing in your own life. When you are faced with a choice, do you actually behave like a person who holds the values you claim to? If you've placed one value as a priority over all others, is that actually reflected in the amount of time, money, and energy you spend on it?

A great way to do this is to actually draw up a chart. Put all your values in a column on the left, and in a column on the right, rate from one to ten your level of satisfaction on this value. If you prize art, beauty, and poetic expression, for example, do you feel that this need/value of yours is in reality fulfilled? Rate all your values this way, remembering that you want to be honest and judgmental—no point in lying to yourself or pretending.

You can probably guess what this list will allow you to do next. Take a look at your ratings. For the lowest ranking, can you write down, in a third column, some concrete actions you can take to bring that value more into your life? If you can do this, you might notice something magical—you have suddenly given yourself a smart, data-driven way to answer the question, "What should I do and what do I want from life?" You already know that if you take action toward any of these unfulfilled values, you are guaranteed to increase your sense of meaning and purpose. What a powerful tool to have!

From *here*, you can begin to turn your mind to goals. The goals you make from this point in the process will be properly informed by what truly matters to you in your life. Let's say you notice that you value knowledge and learning, but are embarrassed to find that, even though you've ranked it as one of your top three values, you can't even remember the last time you did something to satisfy that need. You immediately set some goals for yourself: you sign up for a philosophy course, buy a few fun novels and commit to a daily reading quota, or sign up to learn a skill or craft you've always wanted to learn. These actions might feel a little scary, especially if you are taking a big step out of your comfort zone, but they should in a broad sense feel *right*—they should feel like you are taking the right step in the right direction.

Keep this chart somewhere safe, and return to it in a few weeks or months to check on your progress. How do you rate your expression and fulfillment of a certain value now, after achieving some goals? What adjustments can you make? Don't be too surprised to find that you need to reorder your values or drop a few completely. Sometimes, only practical experience will teach us what is real and what is just illusion. This is something to celebrate—as you fine tune your list, you are getting closer and closer to your genuine self, and trimming away at the false self.

Your Values: A Powerful Decision-Making Tool

As we've seen, values are living things; they are practical, action-based principles. And one of the most practical ways to bring them to life is to allow them to guide and shape your decision-making process. There are two ways to do this. The first is to ask yourself, "How would a person with my values behave in this situation?"

For example, you're someone whohas discovered that you derive enormous satisfaction and meaning out of being diligent, hard working, and dedicated. You feel proud when you start something and finish it, no matter what. You are happiest when you think of yourself as someone who follows through, and who keeps their word. You value integrity.

Along comes a choice one day. In this case, it's just a small choice: the decision between cutting corners on a project where it won't really matter, or doing a proper, complete job even though it would take a little more time and energy. If you value integrity, the right choice is obvious: you do the job well. Not because of the external rewards or pressures, but because you already know that *you* value doing a good job. Naturally, if you were a different person with different values, the "right" choice might be exactly the opposite one.

The second way to use values to help with decision-making is to consciously imagine the *outcome* of certain choices in the future, and then weigh up this outcome against your list of prioritized values. This works a little better for bigger decisions that play out in the long term. For example, you might be wondering whether to accept a new job offer.

You carefully imagine what your life would look like one, two, or five years in the future if you accept this offer. You try to imagine all the effects this will have on your finances, your family life, your lifestyle in general, your career, and so on. Take your time exploring this potential future. Now, from this position, inside your future vision, take another look at your values list. Living your future life, does your satisfaction rating for any of your values go up or down?

Maybe you see that your financial situation would improve, but actually, financial wealth is not a value on your list. You notice also that the new job would have you move further away from family, and spend more time in the office. This would negatively affect your identified value of family time, parenting, and a happy home life. On the other hand, your future self will also experience a boost in occupational fulfillment—which is on your list.

So, what decision do you make? Because you have ranked your values, you can see that career achievement is important to you, but it's not as important as a happy family life. So, your decision is made. You don't take the job. You do this with full knowledge not just of how the job will affect you, but how it will affect your values. You know that the choice you make is one that brings you closer to your fulfilled, properly aligned, and contented self, and further away from a false self (i.e. the one that knows that the job is "once in a lifetime" and that all your friends will think you're crazy for turning it down . . .)

It's likely that you will have some values that conflict with each other. Like the person who values his family but ignores them nonetheless, we can value our career and family both at the same time. In such cases, a simple ranking won't always help us. We might *generally* value one over the other, but that does not mean we should choose the thing we value more every single time. This is true even when we don't have value conflicts like these. Decision-making is an active process; we can't simply compile certain values and rely on a ranking to have every choice pre-decided for us. While a ranking chart is a good general guide to what we should do, we still need to make decisions on a case-by-case basis.

Coming back to the value conflict, the best way to resolve this clash is to take a balanced approach. You can prioritize family on some occasions, and your career on others. If there is something preventing you from doing this, maybe your time management, attempt to work on those issues so that you don't feel like you're skimping on one thing you value for another.

The examples we've discussed here are necessarily small and quite simple. But it's hard to overstate just how much your life can change when you apply your values list consistently. When you are guided by your core values, you have a certain gravity and weight to your character. You have direction and purpose. You can more easily bear difficulty and are more resilient because your energy and attention is focused on one point, rather than being diffuse and reactive.

It may seem like a simple solution, but in the end, we are what we value. A well-considered values list is a tool that clarifies our will and intention, motivates and inspires us, and keeps us going in difficult or confusing times. By now you can probably see that the problem we call "not knowing yourself" is more accurately the problem of "not knowing what you care about."

Takeaways

- A value is a rule, principle, or belief that gives meaning to your life. It is usually something you consider very important in life and base many of your decisions around. This is why when you're confused about what to do in a certain situation or circumstances that you find yourself in, the cause is usually a lack of clarity on what your real values are.
- If you're not sure what your values are in life, don't worry; discovering them is

not hard. However, the process does take time, and you won't simply wake up tomorrow with complete knowledge of what your values are.

- The first step to discovering what your values are is to simply abandon all preconceived notions you have of who you are. Often, the values we have been living by are actually derived externally. This can be through our family, culture, historical era, etc. By starting from a clean slate, we avoid such influences from clouding our judgment regarding our true values.

- Next, think about the things that you feel most strongly about. This could be personal success, close family bonds, serving others in the form of social work, etc. Finding one will often lead you to other values you hold because they point to a "higher" value you possess. Thus, valuing family over career means that your interpersonal relationships in general are valuable to you.

- Once you have a complete list of values, think about your goals in life and how your values align with them. Are the things you're doing now in conjunction with your values and goals? If not, think of ways you can change that and live a life that is truer to your real self.

- As you discover your values, doing actions that promote them will help you decide what it is that you really consider important.

Chapter 2. The Big Five Personality Traits

Chances are, at some point in your life, you've taken a personality, career aptitude, or relationship test to learn more about yourself. The quest to find out what makes human beings tick is as universal as the desire to understand why. What makes some people behave, think, and feel certain ways and not others? Why do humans engage in habitual patterns, even when those could be to their detriment?

The answer may lie in the Big Five personality traits, a theory that dissects the human psyche into five broad characteristics. These five simple factors could determine the very complex question you've been chasing: what makes you *you*?

It's a theory that dates back to 1949, in research published by D.W. Fiske. Since then, it's been gaining popularity and has been written about by the likes of Norman (1967), Smith (1967), Goldberg (1981), and McCrae and Costa (1987). Even though the Myer-Briggs test is one you're more likely to have heard of, the Big Five model is the most widely accepted personality theory in the scientific community today.

Instead of evaluating you as a whole, this is one of the first personality theories to break you down into five traits: openness to experience, conscientiousness, extroversion, agreeableness, and neuroticism. While many personality theories place you on either side of a binary—they say you're either an extrovert or an introvert—the Big Five model presents a spectrum between these five qualities and their opposites. These opposites are closed to experience, spontaneous, introversion, disagreeableness, and stability, respectively.

You may have heard of these before. Terms like introvert and extrovert are thrown around a lot these days, but what do they really mean? They're two ends of the spectrum. Each trait has two extremes, and although we may not want to admit it, every one of us embodies all of these five traits to some degree.

According to this theory, it's how much of each and where we land in the range between the extremes that determine our unique personality. Let's break it down.

In thinking about our own quest for self-knowledge, we can become more familiar with personality theories like this one as a way to better understand humans in general, and ourselves relative to them. It's a little like imagining a person as a unique recipe composed of varying quantities of certain ingredients. The presence of the ingredients is the same for all human beings, but how much of each characteristic you possess as an individual can say a lot about you. As you read about these "personality ingredients," try to see how much of each is in your own makeup, and what insights you can gain from thinking about yourself this way.

Openness to Experience

The first of the Big Five personality traits determines how willing you are to take risks or try something new. Would you ever jump out of a plane? How about pack up and move halfway around the world to immerse yourself in a new culture? If your answer to both of those questions was a resounding yes, then you probably score high in your openness to experience. That is, you seek out the unknown.

At one extreme, people who are high in openness are curious and imaginative. They go in search of new adventures and experiences. They can get bored easily and turn to their creativity to uncover new interests and even daring activities. These people are flexible and seek out variety in their daily life. For them, routine is not an option.

At the other end of the spectrum, people who are low on the openness scale prefer continuity and stability to change. They are practical, sensible, and more conventional than their peers. Change is not their friend.

In the real world, most people fall somewhere in between these opposites, but where you find yourself on the spectrum could reveal a lot about who you are and what you excel at.

Do you dream of being a CEO or at the head of your field, for instance? Openness has been linked to leadership. If you're able to entertain new ideas, think outside the box, and adapt quickly to new situations, you're more likely to become and succeed as a leader (Lebowit, 2016).

It was Apple co-founder Steve Jobs's decision to audit a calligraphy class in 1973 that would lead to the groundbreaking typography in Mac computers years later. At the time, no one associated computers with beautiful fonts, but Jobs saw something that no one else could. He embraced the calligraphy class, sought to change the way people thought about computers, and opened himself up to a new vision of the future.

People who are open also tend to embrace universalism, seeing values as equally applicable to all people (Douglas, Bore & Munro, 2016). They choose peace and tolerance over conflict and discrimination. They see all people as similarly deserving of justice and equality. And they may pursue careers that lead them to fight for their ideals.

A quick look back over your life may reveal just how open to experience you are and how much of this trait you possess. Think of the time you were with your friends and one of them suggested doing something completely crazy and out of the box. What was your reaction? Was it hesitation or excitement? If it was the latter, you are leaning toward openness rather than the opposite.

Conscientiousness

Idealism, creativity, and thirst for new experiences can take you far in life, but how hard you're willing to work for your goals is another determinant of your success. That's where the second Big Five comes in: conscientiousness. This is the personality trait that makes you careful and cautious. You're vigilant in your actions and often think twice, or three times, before making a decision, especially if it wasn't in your original plans.

People who have high levels of conscientiousness tend to be extremely focused on their goals. They plan things out, focusing on the detailed tasks at hand, and they stick to their schedules. They have better control over their impulses, emotions, and behaviors, such that they are able to focus more of their energy on their professional success. While they may not live as adventurously as their peers, they do tend to live longer, thanks in part to their healthier habits.

At the other end of the spectrum, people who are not so conscientious tend to be more impulsive and disorganized. They become demotivated by too much structure, can procrastinate on important work, and have a weaker ability to control their behavior. This can lead to more self-destructive habits, such as smoking and substance abuse, and an overall inability to get things done. Impulse control is no easy feat for them.

So how conscientious are you? Do you like schedules at work but still find yourself avoiding exercise when you get home? You may embrace some aspects of conscientiousness, like schedules and to-do lists, and not others, like exercising or performing other healthy habits. Most people land somewhere in the middle of the conscientiousness spectrum, but if you can find ways to embrace planning and order a little bit more, you could be setting yourself up for success.

Conscientiousness has been linked to better success after training (Woods, Patterson, Koczwara & Sofat, 2016), more effective job performance (Barrick & Mount, 1991), higher job satisfaction, and careers with greater prestige and higher incomes (Judge, Higgins, Thoresen & Barrick, 1999). A study by Soldz and Vaillant (1999) also found that high levels of conscientiousness have helped people better adjust to the challenges of life that will inevitably sneak up on you.

Say, just as you're leaving the office for the day, a colleague comes with another task that he needs urgently. How would you react? If you decide to stay a few more minutes, complete the task, and take your delay in stride, you likely rank higher on the conscientious scale. But if you are already overwhelmed with work as it is and don't see how you can get it done, you may fall toward the other extreme.

Conscientiousness is the preventative medicine we could all use to stop problems before they start. However, too much conscientiousness can also be a bad thing. Such people can easily become overly rigid and dull to be around. They can also be prone to burnout due to the value they place on working hard. Still, conscientiousness is a highly desirable trait overall, one we should all attempt to inculcate in ourselves.

Extroversion

When problems do arise, enthusiasm and optimism are two characteristics that can help carry you through, and that's where extroversion comes in—the third of the Big Five traits. This is the trait that defines how outgoing or social you are.

Extroverts are easy to spot. They're the life of the party, they've got lots of energy, and they know how to talk. Extroverts draw their energy from being around other people, and thrive on being the center of attention. For that reason, they maintain a wide circle of friends and take every opportunity to meet new people.

At the other extreme are people who often find extroverts exhausting to be around: introverts. Why spend time trying to make conversation with large groups of people when you can be at home with your own thoughts? Introverts aren't shy; they simply prefer solitude to socializing or calm to chaos.

Do you wish office parties would never end, or do you feel drained after about an hour? Do you enjoy meeting new people, or would you prefer to be cuddled up at home with a good book? Are you a morning person, or do you truly wake up when the sun goes down?

If you're often the last one to leave a social gathering, you enjoy being around people, and you thrive on the late-night hours, you likely rank high on the extroversion scale. If, on the other hand, you dread the thought of going to parties, would rather stay home alone, and prefer to wake up bright and early to start your day, you're probably more of an introvert.

Depending on the day, you may be inclined to go either way. However, by and large, people typically place somewhere along the spectrum between the two. And while it might have once been thought that those who wake up early and keep to themselves were prone to be more successful, extroversion is actually a strong predictor of who will be a leader (Barrick & Mount, 1991).

Think about it: if you're comfortable being around people, they're more likely to be comfortable around you. If you like starting conversations, you could find yourself with a wider social network in which to mobilize. And if you're more assertive, people might be more prone to believe in you. Moreover, because extroverts thrive on social approval, they are more likely to work hard in order to improve their standing among peers. These are all the makings of a successful leader.

That's not to say that introverts can't lead. It may just require taking a few more steps outside of their comfort zone. However, it's often the case that introverts are simply not interested in being leaders. Introverts do not prioritize status or social approval, and more than happy when others take the rein. For them, it's a waste of energy that could be much better utilized in their own personal endeavors.

Agreeableness

When you're stepping out of your comfort zone, it never hurts to have a helping hand or someone to encourage you along the way. These kinds of people rank high on the agreeableness scale—the fourth of the Big Five personality traits. This is the trait that identifies how kind and sympathetic you are and how warm and cooperative you are with others.

Do you tend to take a big interest in other people and their problems? When you see others going through difficulties, does it affect you, too? If you're empathetic and caring toward others and driven by the desire to help, you may be quite an agreeable person. You feel their pain and are driven to do something about it.

At the other end of the spectrum, people who are less agreeable may find they take less of an interest in other people's lives. Instead of trying to work together to solve a problem, they may be more content to go it alone. Because of their nature, they may often be perceived as offensive or unpleasant to be around.

We all have different thresholds for how much we're willing to do for others and how much we're willing to work together. That limit is where you rank on the agreeableness spectrum.

Why people are so agreeable is still up for debate. For some, it's the genuine concern for the well-being of others. For others, it's the result of social pressure and accepted norms. Fear of consequences can be a motivating factor. Some agreeable people may be acting that way because they are petrified of social confrontation. Whatever the case, research has shown that agreeable people are rarely cruel, ruthless, or selfish (Roccas, Sagiv, Schwartz & Knafo, 2002). However, this also means that agreeable people generally do worse when it comes to their careers. This is easy to see. For example, an agreeable person is much less likely to take up the issue of low pay, whereas a disagreeable person will probably tell their boss they deserve more.

If you're looking for ways to be a little bit happier, figuring out where you lie on the agreeable index may be a good way to start. It's easy to stereotype disagreeable people as simply selfish and unempathetic, but things aren't that simple. While it is true that disagreeable people are more likely to be that way, the thing that makes them so is their reduced sensitivity to conflict, not an innate lack of feelings. These are the people who are unafraid to hold unpopular views, who will give you a piece of their mind if they feel you deserve it, and aren't always swayed by appeals to emotions.

You might believe that it's simply "nicer" to be agreeable, but that isn't necessarily the case. Agreeable people are generally perceived more favorably by others, but this comes at the cost of being unable to assert their own needs. This doesn't just impact their professional lives in the form of lower pay, lower titles, and lower status. It pervades other aspects of life such as relationships too. Disagreeable people might prioritize their own interests above others, but this does not automatically make them less nice.

Neuroticism

We all have those days when nothing is how it seems. You think your coworkers are out to get you. You're so anxious you can't sleep. You feel like you're caught in a Woody Allen film. But if you find yourself having lots of those days, to the point where you feel more down than you do up, you may have high levels of the last of the Big Five traits: neuroticism. This is the personality trait that essentially measures how emotionally stable you are. It identifies your ability to remain steady and balanced versus anxious, insecure, or depressed.

Neurotics tend to approach life with a high dose of anxiety. They worry more than most, and their moods can shift quickly and with little prompting. This kind of behavior can make them prone to being stressed or even depressed.

Those on the less neurotic side of the spectrum tend to be more emotionally stable. When stress comes their way, they have an easier time dealing with it. Bouts of sadness are few and far between, and they see fewer reasons to stress about whatever may come their way. For some, this can be a virtual superpower. Even major stressors like losing a job, getting a divorce, etc., aren't likely to phase stable people too much. However, being too low in neuroticism may also lead to underestimating harms in different situations and being overly optimistic even when it isn't warranted.

Do you find yourself using humor to cope with a challenge, or do problems tend to stress you out? Are you pretty levelheaded all day long, or do you switch from hot to cold in a heartbeat? If you take things in stride and usually only have one mood per day, you're probably less neurotic than others. But if you have many moods in the space of a short amount of time and are anxious more often than not, you're probably on the more neurotic side.

We all fall somewhere along this spectrum, but how you answer these questions is a good indication of which way you lean.

If you're higher on the neurotic scale, you're more likely to suffer from poor job performance, and it may take more to get you motivated (Judge & Ilies, 2002). Setting goals for yourself and sticking to them can be a challenge.

However, being neurotic doesn't have to be all doom and gloom. After all, worrying about our health is what keeps us taking vitamins and visiting the doctor's office for checkups. Neurotics are less likely to ignore the dangers or pitfalls with every decision, ensuring that they have more realistic outlooks on things. In that case, neurotics may actually be one step ahead.

The Big Five Winning Formula

If the human psyche has been narrowed down to five key components, does it follow that there's a winning formula? Is there an ideal combination of traits that every human being should possess to be truly happy?

The answer is yes and no.

It certainly appears that some traits do make you happier than others. Some traits may even make you live longer. But personality is complex, and new scientific discoveries continue to emerge that often challenge preexisting views. Personality can also change over time, so the extent to which people can optimize themselves and cultivate the ideal combination of traits—if it exists—may be limited. But if you're willing to try, here are some hacks that may help.

Don't Want to Be Sick? Try Being More Extroverted.

As a child, did you love to get dirty? Did you get mud all over yourself without any thought to germs—or who was going to do the laundry? Don't tell your own kids or you could be stuck washing clothes for the next three weeks, but you may have actually been on to something. As it turns out, some germs are good for you, and the more you're exposed to them, the more your body gets used to dealing with them.

According to a study led by Professor Kavita Vedhara, extroverts were linked to an increased expression of pro-inflammatory genes, while people ranking high in conscientiousness were associated with a lower expression of these genes. In other words, people ranking higher on the extrovert scale were biologically less susceptible to disease.

That's where being more extroverted can help you. The more people you see, the more you're exposed to a bigger network of germs and possible infections, and the more your body learns to cope. While practicing good hygiene is important, some bacteria can actually toughen up our bodies to diseases.

On the other hand, the more time you spend alone, the less prepared your body is to battle new germs once they come. Being too clean could actually hurt you. The size of your circle of friends, therefore, could actually be a good indicator of the strength of your immune system.

So if you want to be sick less often, try being more extroverted. That means trying to be more comfortable around others and opening yourself up to greater social opportunities. Think of people as germs— you need exposure to some if you're going to stay healthy!

You can start by practicing short conversations with strangers. Next time you visit your local coffee shop, ask your server how their day is going. When you take a taxi, ask your cab driver if it's been a busy night. The more you practice starting conversations, the more natural it will feel and the easier it will become.

Once you've got the gift of the gab, go out and use it. Say yes to dinner invitations you would normally refuse, or invite your friends over to your house more often. Stay off your cell phone in public and see if there's an opportunity to meet someone while you're on the street or waiting for the bus. Sign up for your local Toastmasters club and practice public speaking with other people who also want to improve.

It can be nerve-racking at first to step outside your comfort zone. But if you take baby steps, set yourself incremental goals, and accept any failures as lessons on the path to success, you could be setting yourself up for a more extroverted—and healthier—future in no time.

Want to Live Longer? Be More Conscientious.

When you go on vacation, are you the type to fly by the seat of your pants and book nothing but the plane ticket there? Or do you prefer to know where you're staying, how you'll get there, and what you'll be doing every day thereafter until you return home?

If you're the former, you may be seeking out more excitement in the short term but, in reality, cutting back your adventure in the end. That's because people who are more conscientious—that is, they are more organized and prefer planning over spontaneity—are actually known to live longer.

According to a seventy-five-year longitudinal study by Joshua Jackson (2015), which followed a group of couples in their mid-twenties, men with higher levels of conscientiousness were found to live longer. That's because people high in this trait were more organized, self-disciplined, and prepared. They did fewer things that were spontaneous and more things that were safer. Conscientiousness, therefore, helped them reach riper old ages.

So it turns out that safety pays off. On top of being more organized, high-conscientious people are more self-disciplined and dependable. Even when they dream of taking risks, they convince themselves that it's not in their best interests They stick to their plans and, as a result, do fewer potentially life-threatening things.

If you want to live longer, you could try to be more conscientious. First, get organized about your tasks and your priorities. These days, there are lots of apps that can help you manage your time.

Once you know what needs to be done, you can train yourself to better focus on achieving it. Try meditating for even ten minutes a day. You may find that, over time, you're distracted less and concentrating more on the tasks at hand.

Finally, remember that you don't need to go cold turkey. One step at a time, you may find yourself living a more mindful, determined, and possibly even longer life.

Want a Healthier Heart? Be More Agreeable.

When you're in a good mood, how do you— your body, that is—feel? Does it feel light and energetic, or does it feel heavy and tired? The odds are that when you're in a good mood, so is your body.

As it turns out, the saying that good things happen to good people might actually be true. People who rank high on the agreeableness scale—that is, they're friendly, more compassionate, and looking to get along with everyone—do in fact have healthier hearts versus their more pessimistic peers.

What's the science behind it? According to Bibbey (2013), the less agreeable you are, the weaker your biological stress reactivity—or how your body manages stress. The more relaxed and optimistic you are, and the more you're able to take things in stride, the less stress there is on your heart. That means a healthier heart will keep beating longer. Being more agreeable, therefore, means that your heart is in a much better state.

Now, there are several steps you can take to be more agreeable. First, when you wake up in the morning, tell yourself that you're going to be agreeable with every single person you talk to that day. Go out of your way to be nice to people and to actively listen to them.

Second, try getting involved in volunteer work. Spend some time at your local charity. Seeing those less fortunate than us can bring a better perspective on our own lives.

Finally, practice the art of compromise. If you're adamant about something going your way, you may be alienating everyone else who's involved. But if you're willing to show understanding and put the interest of others above your own, you may just be building a more solid social network to support you down the road.

It may seem hard, but being more agreeable is really just about being more empathetic and less combative with the people you come across. Trying to bring a little more pleasantness, decency, and humbleness to your demeanor can work wonders not only on your social life, but also on your health.

Want to be Happier? Be More Open to Experience.

The last time you tried something new, how did you feel? Maybe it was eating sushi for the first time or taking a dance class. Chances are, even if you didn't like it, you were proud of yourself for taking that step. As it turns out, it may be worth taking a few more of those steps. People who are more open to experience might just be happier overall.

What's the reason? Open people are by nature more curious. Sensitive to beauty, they have a deeper appreciation for art. They're also more in tune with their emotions, and they think and act in ways that may not necessarily conform to society. All of that is to say that they seek out things that make them happy.

At the end of the day, trying new things is good for us. But being open to experience doesn't have to mean jumping out of planes. There are several ways you can discover new things that don't put your life at risk.

First, recognize where your comfort zone is and then step outside of it. Do you like exercising but are afraid of going to the gym? Try a low-key yoga class to get started.

Second, don't worry about what the world around you will think. Have you always wanted to try online dating but were too afraid? Just think, everyone else you'll meet is doing the exact same thing.

Finally, remember that life is short. You may wind up regretting all the things you never tried when it's too late to start.

Being more open to experience can bring you more of the things you've always wanted—and happiness along the way.

Want to Be More in Control? Try Being a Little Less Neurotic.

When was the last time you second-guessed yourself? That never-ending cycle of doubt, wondering if you made the right choice, was likely worse punishment than either choice you could have made. Neuroticism can lead people to do many things, but at the heart of it is the inability to control your thoughts and emotions. Being a little less neurotic may just give you a little more control over yourself, your actions, and, in the end, your overall well-being.

Neurotic people are intense, emotionally speaking. They respond to things in ways that most people wouldn't. They're prone to seeing the challenge, the hopelessness, and the threat that lies in everyday situations. Their negative reactions can go on for longer than others, leaving them in frequent bad moods.

Neurotic people can be prone to vulnerability, leaving them panicked, confused, and helpless under stress. They can suffer intense anxiety and live with a constant fear of something dangerous happening. And they can be sensitive to the perceived judgments of others, leaving them shy, uncomfortable, and even ashamed.

When they're in that state, it can be hard to think clearly, to know what to do, and to handle the situation effectively. That can be a challenging and very likely unhealthy way to live.

On the other hand, if you're able to maintain your calm, poise, and confidence when you're stressed, you become less vulnerable to outside stress. You're less anxious about what may happen next, and you're able to embrace the unknown instead of fear it. You're also not worried about other people watching or judging you.

So how do you become less neurotic?

It may sound grim, but start by reflecting on your own mortality. Once you realize you won't be around forever—and neither will anyone else—you can start to chip away at your neuroses and focus on enjoying the moment.

Next, work out. Exercise can release chemicals in the brain that boost your mood and can go a long way to helping you deal with any anxiety.

Finally, recognize your triggers and try to avoid them. If the same person or situations are always making you anxious or stressed, the easiest solution is to avoid them. Find people and places that help you relax.

Being a little neurotic can be a good thing. But if you find you're not as in control of your emotions as you'd like, challenging your neuroses could lead you to a better, more relaxed state of mind.

All of the above may make it seem pretty simple to just alter aspects of our personality, as though we were fine-tuning a dial up or down. Naturally, the Big Five traits are the broadest categories we can draw for human behavior—they don't tell us how those traits interact, how they come together to form a unique whole, or how they change with time.

Whether you find the Big Five personality trait model useful or not, it can be illuminating to think about your personality in terms of separate quantities. In other words, one way to answer the question of *who you are* is to answer the question, *what are you made of?* This model is also useful because it can shape your attempts to improve. For example, you might take a look at your strong introversion and realize that it's the reason you're unhappy at your job. Or you might realize that you are far more open to experience than you give yourself credit for, and that maybe it's time to appreciate and develop this side of yourself more.

Takeaways:

- The Big Five personality traits are one of the first attempts to classify people based on specific traits rather than as a whole. You can remember the traits easily with the acronym OCEAN: openness to experience (trying new things), conscientiousness (being cautious and careful), extroversion (drawing energy from others and social situations), agreeableness (warm and sympathetic), and neuroticism (anxious and high-strung).
- Each attribute in the OCEAN acronym has some advantages and disadvantages. For example, being neurotic makes you highly prone to stress and anxiety, but it also leads you to realistically evaluate situations and problems better. Being agreeable generally ensures that you are well-liked, but it means you might be less successful professionally.
- Extroverts generally experience more positive experiences and are renowned for being the life of the party. However, they can also be exhausting to be around, especially for introverts. Being conscientious makes it very easy to

pursue and fulfil your goals, have a structured routine, and acquire higher social status. But if you're too high on this trait, it might also make you boring and dull because you aren't spontaneous enough. Lastly, openness to experience means that you're constantly experiencing new and exciting things in your life. However, it also makes it easy for you to struggle with routine since you need higher levels of stimulation to remain interested in what you're doing.

- Unlike other assessments in this book, there have actually been determined to be a winning formula for these traits— not per se, but if you display certain traits, you are more likely to have better mental health and increased happiness. If you are more of the first four traits (OCEA) and less neurotic, you will tend to be happier and more fulfilled in life. It's not hard to understand why—you'll have more experiences, you'll live longer from your caution, you'll have a wider social circle and support system, you'll get along better with others, and you'll be less anxious and more relaxed.

Chapter 3. The Stories We Create

So far, we've looked at a few different ways to tackle the eternal question: who am I?

First, we explored all the ways in which our true self comes down to the values we not only hold, but express in the world. Then, we looked at this abstract and complicated thing called the "personality" and examined one of the most popular personality theories to find that our self might be more or less the sum of various characteristics and traits. Now, we'll look at the question from yet another perspective, i.e. that our self is the result of our ongoing inner narratives.

In this chapter, the focus is geared toward gaining insight about ourselves based on stories we might tell ourselves and what those stories might mean. Humans are story-tellers and meaning-makers. That chatter inside your head that is narrating your life as you live it? That's not reality— that's a story. Your belief that you're this or that kind of person? Also a story. Perhaps it's a story you learned and internalized from someone else, or perhaps it's a story you made up in response to your life experience. But we can imagine that stories and narratives are like little stitches of meaning we use to pull together the events in our lives, our hopes, fears, blind spots, and so on.

The way in which we construct (or express) our identities through story has been a favorite theme for psychologists throughout the years. In narrative therapy, for instance, we can use stories to shape and guide our experience, and figuratively *tell ourselves* through story. But we can use the same tools to gain deeper insight into ourselves.

We can use story to find out who we really are.

The overall goal here is to draw meaning from people's subconscious thought. When you ask yourself a pointed question (such as "What makes me happy?"), you likely aren't going to be able to answer that question. Even if you do answer the question, it probably won't be an answer that helps you achieve greater happiness.

There are two methods of interest: the Carl Jung personality test and Kate Wendleton's seven stories exercise. Both seek to evaluate personality based on answers that people give from seemingly innocent questions. Indeed, in a moment, you'll see why they can be seen like both a horoscope or an illuminating look into someone's psyche, depending on who you're talking to.

The Seven Stories Exercise

Kate Wendleton, career counselor, created this exercise out of Bernard Haldane's work in helping military personnel transition into civilian work.

After World War II in the 1940s, the job market began to get flooded with veterans returning home and looking for work. It was very evident that many businesses and organizations didn't possess the resources or skills to capitalize on these veterans' talents and capacities. Veterans were accustomed to jobs that pertained to war. These jobs weren't necessarily available or well known in the general labor force. They simply had no idea how to evaluate them.

Haldane wanted to do something to help the veterans. First, he asked veterans to recollect on their best achievements while at the same time clarifying what they enjoyed doing the most. Next, he helped them clarify their individual strengths and skills that were transferable. Specifically, the focus was to identify ones that could be useful to an employer.

Third, Haldane helped them market and present their offerings in a way that appealed to a potential employer. He would help the employer recognize the benefits of hiring the veterans based on their skills, achievements, and enjoyments.

Although it was deemed to be extremely radical at the time, Haldane's inside-out approach was able to help many veterans who needed assistance in seeking employment. He helped them find their strengths and skills that would eventually make them marketable in the conventional job market. Traditional methods for finding jobs always used an outside-in approach. In other words, old methods would try to fit people into job skills employers were looking for rather than highlighting the individual's real skills to bring to the table.

Initially, Wendleton's exercise was created to help people in the realm of career counseling, but it's become popular to use when people want to identify the joys in their life. Also, it's used to help identify what people need more of in terms of the present and the future. The ultimate goal is to help people discover exactly what they need in order to add more zest and joy to their overall lives.

The seven stories asks people to complete the following steps.

Step One: Write Down Twenty-Five Accomplishments

For this step, people would identify twenty-five accomplishments that they've felt good about doing. This would involve having people reflect on life accomplishments that ranged from childhood all the way to adulthood. The answers should be specific and not just a general statement. Normally, people may have a hard time with this, but they should really just go with their gut. They should write down whatever makes them feel good. Twenty-five is a lot of *anything* to think about, but the point is that you dig deep and leave no stone unturned.

A good tip to follow that will help you achieve this goal is to carry a small notebook around so that you can note things as you remember them. Give yourself at least four to five days to complete this activity.

For instance, someone might write that they were elected class president during their sophomore year in high school, or they coordinated a charity fundraiser selling car wash tickets to benefit the homeless while in their junior year of college.

Step Two: Narrow that Down to Seven Accomplishments

From the list of twenty-five, people should now narrow their list down to the seven most important and significant ones that have made them happy.

For most people, they may choose to elect ones such as overcoming cancer when they were thirty-two years old by actively going to treatment and changing their diets. They might also recall putting together their first furniture all on their own when first moving into their house. Typically, these seven accomplishments are more memorable and significant. Again, there is no definition or criteria for which seven you should use. Chances are you'll be able to figure out which are the most significant to you.

Step Three: Write Stories Associated with Those Seven Accomplishments

Taking from the seven narrowed accomplishments, people are to write out the stories associated with each of them. From here, they should be able to identify the skills and lessons learned and manifested from those experiences. They might be able to connect some dots and make connections to certain pathways that occurred during attainment of those accomplishments. Write the story in the first or third person, and make sure to include the context and the aftermath of how you felt afterward.

When people are able to go through their experiences, they may be able to identify the elements of those experiences and how those elements made them happy. They can see commonalities in those experiences as well as certain aspects that attributed to their happiness. Write out the emotions felt in as much detail as possible, and attempt to reflect in the story why there were such feelings of triumph and happiness. Also note the various skills and abilities you showcased in the process of accomplishing these seven things.

Those who overcame cancer might talk about how they became much more optimistic in their outlooks on life, as well as more resilient when faced with adversity. They remember those agonizing moments of chemotherapy but the great ways that the nursing staff helped them throughout the process. They saw the compassion that medical staff had for patients and, in turn, became more positive and uplifted.

For the people who put together furniture for the first time, they might recall feeling independent and able to follow directions once they really focused their attention to it. They remembered what it felt like to read through instructions that seemed like another language at first. They would also remember that great feeling of tightening that last screw and placing the furniture in the perfect spot in the house. It might sound trivial, but remember, it's about the feelings and emotions it gave you, not about the achievement itself.

Here are some questions you can ask yourself as you craft your stories for these achievements:

- Why did you do that thing, and what was your motivation behind undertaking it?
- Who else was involved, and how did they contribute to your achievements?
- What makes this accomplishment so meaningful to you?

Step Four: Analyze Those Stories

In a deeper purpose, people would now reflect and analyze what they learned from their experiences. Moreover, people can look back on all of their older experiences and attempt to connect them to ones pertaining to the seven stories.

Besides the cancer survivors learning about their feelings after the experience, they were able to analyze their overall feeling of the process. They may discover that all of the experiences, even when negative, happened for a reason, and they were meant to prosper through it all. They reminisce about all the things they used to love to do, like playing soccer or drawing, prior to being diagnosed with their condition. As a result, it motivates them to overcome this ailment and work toward participating in those hobbies again.

The homeowners may learn overall that they truly enjoy the beauty and struggles of homeownership. They start with a piece of furniture and then can feel confident to move on to bigger home projects like tile and floor replacements. They start to walk around the house and notice that the bathroom could get a little bit of a facelift. This motivation to do more because they loved the sense of accomplishment helps them power through their initial fear of not being a "do-it-yourselfer."

Step Five: Two Hundred Possibilities to Achieve Goals

After people have determined what they're good at and love to do, they can come up with two hundred possibilities that would help them carry out these activities. The purpose behind this is to help people get excited about their possibilities. They become more confident and not discouraged if one option doesn't always work out. Plus, it helps reduce people's attachment to just one possibility.

In terms of the cancer survivors, they'd be able to get excited about their newfound health, and identify more steps they can take to stay healthy, such as regular screenings, healthy eating, and reduced exposure to toxins. Homeowners might think about enrolling in some DIY classes at the local hardware store to learn more about building things on their own.

The idea behind the seven stories is to get people to find ways to live their best lives possible based on what they have discovered, and that they truly care about their lives. When people are able to reflect and identify things they've done well, and enjoyed them at the same time, it helps guide them in positive decision-making for their future. Knowing that they have a plethora of options and control over their own actions gives people the chance to be advocates in their own identities and behavior.

You can try out this exercise for yourself or create a different version according to your needs. What's important is that you use story and narrative to draw together all the disparate elements of your life—your past experiences, your strengths, weaknesses, major life events, goals, disappointments— into a narrative that you imbue with meaning.

In seeking to discover ourselves, we can forget that our identity is not fixed, but something that moves and changes with time. In other words, there's a narrative: a beginning, stakes, a middle, rising tension, a main character, and even, if you like, an ending with a moral to the story. When we place ourselves inside a story, we give our lives meaning and context, and we also define more clearly our role within that context. You might feel completely aimless in life and unsure about who you are, but if you sit down and deliberately examine the pieces that make up your life, you can see the bigger narrative arc—and you can even change it, if you want to.

Carl Jung Personality Test

Another popular test used to test personality is that from Carl Jung. Carl Jung was normally very analytical and pluralistic in his thinking. He had a lot of influence from Buddhist ways of thinking, which then translated to the way he viewed and studied people and their personalities. He believed that there was a deeper connection to the way that people thought about simple things.

Although simple things are easier to identify, it's the answers that people provided that would reveal more about the person they were and how they prefer to do things. From how they view other people to how they envision their deaths, the questions from his personality test were very unique and intriguing. It's always been attributed to Carl Jung, but it seems to have gained a lot of popularity from the book *Diary* by Chuck Palahniuk.

The test asks individuals to answer the following.

First, name a color. Any color. Now think of three descriptive adjectives that describe that color.

Second, name an animal. Any animal. Now think of three descriptive adjectives that describe that animal.

Third, name a body of water. Name three descriptive adjectives describing it.

Fourth, imagine you're in a room. All the walls are white and there are no windows or doors. Describe in three descriptive adjectives how that room feels to you. Stop here. Complete the questions. Then read on to see what they could mean about you.

The basis behind each question is where the evaluation and analysis really happens.

Question one: (color choice) the three words represent how you see yourself.
Question two: (animal choice) the three words represent how you see other people.
Question three: (body of water choice) the three words represent your preferred sex life.
The last question: (white room description) the three words represent your death.

Let's take a look at what each question and answer might be revealing. To reiterate, the answers you gave are not the important part; the adjectives you used are.

For instance, someone answers the following:
Teal: happy, cool, calming
Deer: timid, quiet, scared
Waterfall: raging, powerful, strong

White room: calm, tranquil, confusing

According to the test, this person sees themselves as happy, cool, and calming. Meanwhile, they see others as timid, quiet, and scared around them. They view sex as raging, powerful, and strong, and when they think of death, they think of calm, tranquility, and confusion.

Each of these questions has an interesting way of describing people based on the answers they provide. Although people believe they are just answering normal and easy questions, they are providing a deeper indication into who they are as a person.

Overall, this test asks people simple questions that they'd be able to answer, but it does provide a little more insight into the analysis of those answers. They are able to dissect the choices they make for each question and relate those answers to an evaluation of their personalities and identities. It's probably less scientific than anything else in this book, but it does provide food for thought and, at worst, is a great game to play with a date.

Both the seven stories exercise and the Carl Jung personality test are methods that people can use to reflect and analyze their own experiences and behaviors, using the medium of storytelling. The second one taps a little more into the unconscious mind, looking for those inner stories we may tell ourselves that we aren't necessarily aware of. These inner narratives can sometimes be hidden by the false self, by expectation, bias, or habit. But in bringing these associations out into the open, we learn more about how we have been unconsciously constructing and experiencing our own identity. For example, you might never have told anyone directly that your ideal sex life is "raging and powerful," but if you ask the question obliquely, you might be surprised to see just how honest your answers are!

From there, you can better understand your own personality and identity, which helps you become more self-aware. These tests can easily be used to help people take more control over their behavior and personality traits, considering they are more in touch with why they act the way they do.

Takeaways:

- The narratives and stories we tell ourselves about who we are constitute a large part of our sense of self. However, few of us have actually taken the time to sit down and think about the stories we tell ourselves about our achievements, who we are, what we're good at, etc. By reconfiguring and identifying our stories that are grounded in past experiences we've had, we can construct a more coherent identity for ourselves and discover who we really are.
- Sometimes the best way to discover something about ourselves is to ask seemingly innocent questions, then read between the lines. The way we answer these types of questions can be more honest and indicative than intentionally trying to figure out your personality and identity.

- The first way to do this is through the seven stories exercise, which implores you to first note down twenty-five of your most highly coveted achievements. Then, you must narrow it down to get your seven greatest accomplishments and write the stories involved in those triumphs. Try to recall as much detail as you can, and then analyze what these stories really tell you about yourself. Finally, write down two hundred possible ways you can use the results of your analysis to express your values and identity better in the world around you. What comes out in the story will tell you more about who you are and what you seek than trying to answer those questions alone.
- The second method to discover yourself is through Carl Jung's personality test, which consists of four steps: name a color, name an animal, name a body of water, and think about a white room. The ensuing adjectives you use to describe each of those answers will tell you something specific about your personality that your psyche may not

consciously have realized.

Chapter 4. Self-Awareness Questions

Famous Greek philosopher Aristotle (384–322 BC) stated, "Knowing yourself is the beginning of all wisdom," and founding father of the United States of America Benjamin Franklin couldn't have said it better: "There are three things extremely hard: steel, a diamond, and to know one's self." The comparison of self-awareness to that of other "invincible" things factors just how important it was to philosophers in history.

Self-awareness is one of the most sought-after feelings of human existence. Everyone wants to be sure of themselves and know who they are and what they represent. It's not that we are happier with that knowledge—the knowledge itself is neutral. But it's what that knowledge represents that makes us want it.

When we are self-aware, we feel that we are living our best selves, correcting our errors, and seizing our full potential. One of those is probably the reason you picked up this book in the first place. Psychologists and scientists also believe in the need for self-awareness. They view this consciousness as a direct relation to some of the most essential states of being. These states of being are greater happiness, less inner conflict, and more confidence in decision-making.

Greater Happiness

Happiness is not a physical thing that can be defined. Every person has his or her own version of what happiness looks or feels like. But regardless of what it is to each person, the act of achieving it comes from being more self-aware because you know what you want. People are able to express themselves more freely without judgment.

Happiness can look very different to everyone, so understanding oneself allows them to find his or her own version. You may have been following someone else's blueprint or template, but the second you find your own is a moment of triumph.

Less Inner Conflict

When people act upon their inner feelings and values, there may be times when they feel some type of inner conflict with themselves. With a more heightened sense of self, it becomes less likely that inner feelings and outside actions will ever collide. This is especially felt in making decisions.

Regardless of the type of decisions being made—buying a sweater or choosing a life partner—it can almost be guaranteed that decision-making will be that much easier with a stronger, self-aware individual. People will have set personal guidelines they can apply to solve everyday problems and thus make better choices.

So how do we actually gain self-awareness? The focus is geared around having people ask themselves simple and direct questions that hopefully hint at things just outside our conscious knowledge.

Typically, people will analyze and reflect on their nature-versus-nurture upbringing, environments, and social circles to gather their sense of self. They'll ask themselves questions, again, such as, "What makes me happy and fulfilled?" This should be considered a mediocre starting point, because the only type of answer you are going to construct from this is a lovely sounding platitude that doesn't actually give you insight into yourself.

And so, this chapter works to provide a simpler way of achieving self-awareness. No one knows you better than yourself, and sometimes, that's the problem with gaining self-awareness. You may not lie to yourself, but you are privy to all of your own thoughts, whereas others can only observe your actual actions and behaviors—which are what really represent who you are in the world.

Remember, the actual answers to these questions are not the important part. These questions are phrased as they are to challenge and inspire deep thought. They ask people to dive deeper into understanding *why* they answered the way they did, and dig into their behavioral and thought patterns.

1. What kind of prize would I work hardest for, or what punishment would I work hardest to avoid?

The answer to this question might help identify the true motive behind an individual's drive. Beyond surface-level things, what is really motivating people? Is this something they care about? And what type of pain or pleasure matters to them?

On an instinctual level, what really matters the most in both a positive and negative way?

Gamblers all want one prize: the jackpot. They try and try again, whether it be scratchers or slot machines to try to win that big prize money. Is their hope that they will eventually win back all the money they've already spent into their gambling habit? Is their hope to become richer than they can imagine?

Why are they working so hard? You might discover that their motivation is the thrill and rush of the risk involved. Do they care about making steady pay or finding their purpose? Perhaps not. When you can dig into what someone wants the most and why, you can often find what is driving them without having to ask it directly.

When thinking of the prize you'd work hardest for, ask yourself how far you'd go to achieve that prize. This will often reveal the punishment you want to avoid most. A person might value money because to them, that is what success looks like. But what lengths would they go to for money? Would they break the law or cheat and deceive people? Maybe they're fine with being ambitious as long as it stays within some moral and legal bounds.

2. Where do you want to spend money, and where are you fine going cheap or skipping altogether?

This answer may reveal what matters to someone's daily living and what they want to experience or avoid in their lives. There comes a point when material belongings no longer have a meaning or purpose for someone. For example, sometimes, spending money on experiences instead of a new purse has the potential to improve someone's overall well-being and outlook on life.

What do you have no problem splurging on, and what doesn't matter to you? When deciding on vacation finances, people may opt to splurge on a boat trip and stay in a shabby hotel. This reveals their desire to experience an unforgettable moment rather than staying in a nice hotel, what they view as a waste of money. Others might opt for the opposite and revel in their creature comforts while not seeing much of the scenery. In either case, they've used their money to quite literally identify and spend their priorities. Ask yourself whether you prefer spending on experiences or materialistic possessions. Would you go on a tour to Europe, or buy the latest iPhone?

Where your money goes is an important part of what makes you happy, so if you can pay attention to where you let it flow and where you cut it off, you'll immediately know what matters to you on a daily basis.

3. What is your most personally significant and meaningful achievement and also your most meaningful disappointment or failure?

It is pretty common that experiences, whether they're good or bad, shape people into who they are for the present and future. Significant experiences also tend to create their self-identities—*you are this kind of person because you did this and succeeded or failed.* Achievements and failures tie into how someone sees oneself. Overall, it's about how people want to see themselves.

This question will get a response about how people view themselves, good or bad. Failure will evoke flaws they hate, while achievements will bring up strengths they are proud of.

A career woman who has worked her way up the corporate ladder might reflect on her accomplishments. She looks back to the things she did in order to get that corner office. She discovers that her resilience and determination helped her push through obstacles to get to where she is now. The story about her career accomplishments is actually a story about the positive traits she utilized in reaching that point—her self-identity. You can imagine the same negative type of self-identity might unfold if the same woman were to talk about her failures.

The way that people answer this question shows that they can identify positive and negative experiences and dissect why they hold particular values either so high or low.

4. What is effortless and what is always exhausting?

This question is designed to tell you where you should spend your time. Some people are better at things than others. Engineers are great at math, while artists are masters of creativity. Lawyers are great at arguing a point, while teachers do best at inspiring young minds. What might people say about you?

Whatever aspects of life, occupation notwithstanding, come easily and naturally to you are things you should emphasize and capitalize on. The things that are always challenging and exhausting may be worthwhile, but they may also be things you should simply let go of. The way people answer this question should help them tap into their best strengths and areas for improvement.

For instance, as a baker answers this question, she may automatically recognize her creative niche for blending ingredients together to make a beautiful dessert. She will see that although she has practiced perfecting her craft, it has naturally been very easy for as long as she can remember. She just sees outside the box in a way that few other bakers can.

On the other hand, it may take her much longer to write and follow traditional recipes. As she reflects on these natural strengths and weaknesses, she can look at herself and design a career that better suits her strengths and weaknesses instead of trying to conform to other people. This is all because she recognized her natural talents and followed them.

5. If you could design a character in a game, what traits would you emphasize and which would you ignore?

This helps people focus on their ideal selves. Imagine that you have a limited number of points to give a person but six traits to spread the points across. Which will you choose to emphasize and bolster, and which will you choose to leave average or even lacking? It's more than likely that this either represents how you see yourself or how you would like to see yourself. You might even create someone entirely different from who you are.

For someone answering this question, it helps them identify what they consider to be their strengths and flaws. The strengths you can continue to make front and center, while the weaknesses can be pinpointed to be worked on.

6. What charity would you donate millions to if you had to?

Besides reflecting on the needs of oneself, there now comes the test of someone's worldwide view. Asking this question forces one to think about the values and needs of others and what they care about outside of themselves.

Will you donate to an animal shelter or a charity for cancer? Perhaps you would sponsor a child from a third-world country? They all say very different things about you. Whatever the case, it tells you how you want to see the world and what types of causes matter to you.

Another version of this question is to ask what you would do if you won the lottery, or suddenly found that money was no object. Imagine you no longer had to work for money, and think of what you would fill your day with instead. Travel? Community work? Art? Education? Or would you have one big party with your friends and family?

Take the time to imagine your world with all the necessities of money removed, and you may be left with a clearer picture of who you are and what you value beyond practicalities.

7. What activities are so absorbing that you forget to eat or even go to the bathroom?

This tells you what kind of activities you enjoy so much that you get lost in them. The kind of thing you could easily do for hours without even noticing the time go by. It might have been a long time since you had this experience, but think back—when last did you find yourself genuinely surprised at how carried away you had gotten? If you can identify a few activities that have had you feeling this way—what did they all have in common?

Maybe you discover that whenever you work with people, you really get into the flow and can work for ages without getting tired. Maybe being creative gives you that laser focus. Look at these activities, and you're sure to learn more about yourself and what you value.

8. What topics do you never shut up about?

As you can see, many of these questions are asking the same thing in slightly different ways: what topics or activities feel effortless for you? Which things just seem to happen with ease? It's a powerful clue to what is most natural and rewarding for you, whether it's an activity or a particular idea or area of interest.

Can you think of a time someone mentioned something in conversation and you felt like you might burst with everything you had to say on the topic? Imagine someone who could literally yammer away for hours on a topic they were passionate about, and still not feel like they'd covered everything. Identifying the topics that get you riled up in this way can show you where your passions, interests, and strengths lie.

9. What were you obsessed with as a child, and why?

There's a reason many people ask this question when trying to pinpoint life purpose and passion. As children, all of us are filled with a certain sense of hope and possibility that we may lose as adults. We may get so stuck in the stories we tell ourselves or get bogged down in other people's obligations and expectations, that we forget the original passion we came into the world with.

But examining your old childhood hobbies and interests is a powerful way to remind yourself of what used to catch your attention, of how you used to be, before you started telling yourself otherwise. Maybe even as a child you adored writing stories for your teddies, and this reminds you of a lifelong love of writing and a buried dream to be an author.

Maybe you were always active and sporty, and now miss that sense of physical prowess as an adult. Maybe you were more ambitious, more caring, or more artistic as a child. How did you play and who were your friends? You might find a few pieces of your lost identity if you went back and reminded yourself of all these childhood traits. What could you do today that would make your five-year-old self squeal with delight?

10. What would you like to see on your obituary?

Let's take things in the other direction and consider what life will look like as you get closer to the end. If you could magically see your own obituary, or the engraving on your tombstone, what words would you be most happy to see there? What could you read that would make you feel most accomplished and proud of the life you had lived?

Try to pick three things that you would most like to be known for after you die. All of us want to be remembered fondly, but what kind of impact do you most hope to have achieved? Maybe you want people to have considered you a kind, compassionate soul who made other people feel loved. Maybe you want people to admire your achievements and your hard work, and to be remembered as a solid, industrious person who made their mark on their world. Or maybe you most want to be known for the beautiful or creative works you left behind.

11. What would you do if you only had a month left to live?

In keeping with the slightly morbid topics (death does have a way of bringing some things into clearer focus!), ask yourself what you would do if you were diagnosed with a terminal condition that would carry you off after just a month. So often, we allow the noise and nonsense of life to get in the way, and delay asking the big questions because we're so distracted and busy dealing with the smaller things in the here and now.

But in the same way that a near-death experience can suddenly help people see what actually matters to them, this question asks us to cut to the chase. When time is limited, what really counts? Notice if your answer is to live in a way that's very different from the way you live now. What does this enormous discrepancy say about you? Why are you putting off things that you clearly value?

Notice also if there are a few things that you'd immediately forget about if you only had a month left to live. If you barely gave your spouse a second thought, or just automatically assumed you'd walk away from your job, why is that? Some people might imagine themselves finally giving a piece of their minds to people they've been angry with for ages. Others picture themselves confessing long secret feelings of love or calling distant relatives to ask for forgiveness.

This question not only focuses in on what is ultimately important, but it can also show you what distractions or disruptions you might have allowed to creep into your life. When it's literally life or death, there's no time for the false self, for phoniness, or for blindly doing what other people want you to do. Sadly, some people really do leave the personal discovery of their real selves to the last minute, on their death bed. But if you ask this question now, you can hopefully find illuminating answers well before that point!

Being able to ask these questions evokes a deeper connection to one's own values, ideas, and awareness. They influence people to take a step back, think, and wholeheartedly answer questions not typical of finding their identities. Afterward, the hope is that there is some type of action plan component following acknowledgment of their traits and behavior patterns.

The purpose of asking these is to, again, examine behavior. Plus, it helps people see what their personalities and identities are all about. There is a wide range of information that can be discovered through these questions rather than just being a delivery of information itself.

These questions are much more heartfelt and guide a person in thinking about the most relevant aspects of his or her character. These questions make people think beyond predictable statements that organically stimulate more meaningful thought. Then more influence is placed on creating some type of objective to achieve.

When it comes to particular questions, it's good to figure out a plan for achieving next steps and making applicable changes. The questions help to influence and motivate. The person who answers these questions will then capitalize on their revelations and put the plan into action, so to speak.

Then it's also important to remember that it's not only the actual answers that help someone identify their own awareness of himself. The point is to look beyond the answers and read between the lines. Critical thinking, evaluation, and reflection are the key skills at play here.

People must critically analyze their answers and where those answers came from. From there, they need to apply this newfound sense of awareness to further enhance their own quality of life. Where are things going well and what can be improved? Further, how might one get started with applying their realizations as catalysts for change?

Overall, the idea is to improve happiness while eliminating things that make them unhappy. Being self-aware and understanding one's own identity is one of the most important steps toward reaching true happiness.

Remember that happiness is only measurable by each individual. Although happiness comes in different shapes and forms for people, the act of achieving it can be the same for every person who uses these questions to guide them on the right path. The road to happiness is about discovering oneself and learning to formulate a scheme in reaching and sustaining that happiness.

Takeaways:

- Self-awareness is important, but not easily gained. That's why it's so highly valued. Methods like using personality tests and engaging with certain exercises have been taken up in previous chapters. This one is about asking yourself particular questions, the answers to which will reveal major components of who you are and what you truly value in life.

- The best way to gain self-awareness is to ask about your behaviors and actions, not your intentions or thoughts. Your thoughts are too easily corrupted or otherwise simply not representative of what you actually feel. When you can analyze your behaviors and actions, you can then glean real information about yourself.

- There are several questions you can ask yourself. For example, what is one achievement that you're most proud of and one thing you've done that you're most ashamed of? The achievement you're proud of will reveal a lot about what you value, and what kind of skills you are good at that made the achievement possible in the first place. On the other hand, the thing you're ashamed of is something you should be wary about repeating and reminding yourself that you do not want to be the same person who did that horrible thing.

- Another great question is to ask yourself what feels effortless, and what is always exhausting to do. Everyone has something that they're naturally very good at. Discovering what this is in your case can take some trial and error, but the time investment will be worth it. Similarly, the thing you find exhausting is probably not a large part of what you value.

- A third question, among others, is what you would do if you only had one month left to live. Say you've been diagnosed with cancer—what are the things you would stop doing immediately, and what would you do more often with the little time you have left?

- These questions are all vague and have no right answer, but one can immediately see why they're insightful and reveal things about ourselves that we may not have thought about.

Chapter 5. Unconscious Upbringings

In the previous chapters, we've considered identity, personality, and self as more or less contained and isolated phenomena. But of course, no man is an island. To answer the question of who you are, we can look at another related question: where did you come from?

This chapter works to discuss how people's upbringing effect and have direct influence to their personalities, especially in the subconscious manner. Not all of this may be true, but it's safe to say that there is a plethora of research that has yielded some very interesting theories. These tell researchers that it's worth looking into people's childhoods to find clues as to why people act the way they do.

If you want to gain a deeper awareness of who you are as a person, you can gain plenty of insight by examining the home in which you were raised. As you read on about certain theories that focus on family dynamics and early childhood experiences, you might wonder, does our upbringing establish our "false self," or does it truly shape who we are on a deeper level? This is a difficult question to answer, but by the end of the chapter, you'll hopefully agree that whichever it is, the path of self-discovery must include a trip down memory lane to examine our early family history.

Alfred Adler Birth Order Theory

One theory that doesn't have much scientific validation to back it up is the Alfred Adler birth order theory. This proposed theory came from Alfred Adler (1870–1937) as he studied the effect that birth order had on people's personality. By definition, birth order was the order of when a child was born in his or her given family.

For instance, in a family of three, the sequence goes as follows:

The first child is the firstborn.
The second child is the middle born.
The youngest child is the latter or third born.

You may agree at first glance that birth order does seem to create a certain personality type. There's the stereotype that the eldest child must set the example for the other children and has the most pressure from parents to succeed in a conventional manner. That of course means the younger children are allowed to run wild because there is less pressure. This may be true, but the idea of birth order becomes a bit more complex when consideration is placed on the effects of birth order on children's personalities.

According to Adler, the firstborn children would receive a lot of attention from the family. But that attention would last only up until the second child was born. Once the second child came into the picture, the first child would be considered Adler's coined term "dethroned." All of these actions unconsciously influenced the child's personality through adulthood.

Firstborn
Let's take a look at the first child. Adler stated that they will be prone to perfectionism and a constant need for affirmation or validation. This would then translate to them being intellectual, conscientious, and dominant in most social settings. Adler would describe this child as losing their parents' devoted attention with the presence of other children, and they would try to get it back somehow, even if it took their entire life in doing so.

This same child would have expectations set to be a role model for the younger siblings. This child has control of attention from the parents because there is no one else to compete with. Once control of attention is lost on the first child's part, they can have one or several of the following reactions:

- protects themself against forces that can change their destiny
- becomes insecure or extremely conservative
- helps parents when the second child is born

Second Born
Then there are the second born and middle children. Adler's perspective on second-born children was that they grow up sharing attention from caregivers of the firstborn. Since they grew up learning to share this attention, they're more likely to cooperate and be less needy than firstborn children.

Second-born children are able to follow examples set by older siblings. They are usually trying to follow in the footsteps of the eldest children and catch up to them. Because of this, Adler believed that second-born children were more likely to adjust to life in general than the other children. This child is also prone to being dethroned if another child is born afterward.

Adler refers to the second born as the "peacemaker." Because the firstborn came before them, this might prompt them to be competitive, rebellious, and always wanting to be the best at everything. They might struggle with trying to figure out their place in the family, then later in the world.

Second-born children are eager for praise from their parents, and they often develop keen traits in arts or academia to compensate for this goal. If they are the middle children, they tend to be more flexible and diplomatic than other members of the family.

Last Born
These children are the babies of the family. The baby can never be dethroned by another sibling. They don't really have any followers but can be considered antagonistic toward other siblings because

they become the center of attention for an extended number of years without competition.

Typically, the baby will get most of the attention in families. This is largely due to the other siblings moving on in their stages of life. They will have developed their own sense of independence without having to rely on their parents. Thus, this results in leaving all of the attention to the youngest child, the last born.

According to Adler, the youngest child also tends to be dependent and selfish. This happens because they have always been taken care of by other family members and not necessarily through any fault of their own. The last born can also possess positive traits such as confidence, socializing, and the ability to have fun. They are the only children who don't have to fight for attention from their parents.

They will, though, have difficulty with authority, especially when they are told no. Going to school is a hard transition because they have to shift their focus to the teacher. Adler did express that these children would be more mature and feel more comfortable around others versus other children.

Only Child
So what about the only child? This is the one type that is still difficult to completely evaluate when it comes to the development of personality types. Researchers have indicated the only child has tendencies to develop first-born characteristics. Others have said that an only child could be classified in any of the birth order personalities. For instance, the only child can have the same characteristics as the middle child or the last born.

When it comes to birth order, it's not a matter of choice and subconscious. It can affect people's identities simply from the basis of chance and when someone is born in the family. Because of this, it allows people to gauge a better understanding into who they are and why they act the way they do based on their order in their families.

Attachment Theory

Attachment theory is another theory where unconscious happenings during childhood affect people well into adulthood.

Based on research started by John Bowlby, notably continued by Mary Ainsworth, then by Bartholomew and Horowitz, there are four main attachment styles, or ways we approach emotional attachment to other people. These patterns usually begin with children's relationships to their parents or caretakers, and persist into adulthood where they influence adult relationships.

According to Bowlby, the theory essentially forces the child to unconsciously ask whether the caretaking figure is nearby and attentive. If the child perceives the answer to this question to be yes, he will feel loved, secure, and confident. As a result, the child will feel confident to explore and have a degree of physical and mental separation from the caretaker. However, if the child perceives the answer to be no, the child will experience anxiety and become fearful whenever the caretaker is not in their immediate vicinity. These feelings form the basis for the attachment styles.

The four attachment styles are:

1. Secure
2. Anxious-preoccupied
3. Dismissive-avoidant
4. Fearful-avoidant

Secure Attachment

As much as we would like to think that secure attachment is the most common attachment style, it absolutely is not. And there's a reason the other three attachment styles have somewhat ominous names.

People with secure attachment styles are emotionally balanced and have a history of warm and caring interactions that began in childhood. They don't approach people out of fear. Instead, they have a strong sense of self and look for the positive in any relationship.

They have a healthy range of positive and negative emotions, and are less prone to emotional outbursts because they are secure. They may be independent or relatively dependent, but it's a conscious choice and not based on anxiety or fear.

They aren't emotionally repressed and can express their emotional closeness and attachment with little or no trouble. Securely attached people feel comfortable with intimacy. They do not view it as a threat. They do not feel that intimacy is completely dependent on their partner or that it robs them of their independence. Instead, they understand that when they enter into a relationship, a third party is born—the relationship.

Not surprisingly, these people are able to be warm and loving. Again, love is defined as you giving, not taking. Anxious people define love as taking.

The biggest difference between securely attached people and other types of people is their lack of insecurity. This allows them to open themselves to others yet give others space when it is needed.

How do they act in relationships?

Just imagine how someone who is secure and confident in their relationship acts. They are not jealous or possessive, and they don't have nightmares about being cheated on. They are attentive but relaxed, and generally allow independence and freedom because they don't feel they have anything to worry about.

Various studies report that people with this attachment style are happier and more fulfilled in their relationships, and that's no surprise. Imagine what a relationship where the sanctity of the relationship was never in question would be like. Some people never get to that point.

If you want this chapter to be anything more than a series of "Oh, that's interesting" moments, you should take a moment to honestly assess how much each of these attachment styles resonates with you. Don't

36

make the mistake of assuming that your attachment style is automatically secure or healthy.

If you don't take the time to diagnose yourself, and you subsequently attempt to remedy or fix a problem with your relationships, it's like taking a random medication to treat an illness. It doesn't make sense to do that. And yes, loving others does indeed start with loving yourself.

Anxious-Preoccupied Attachment

This is the first type of insecure attachment, and it is defined by anxiety and preoccupation with the relationship.

People with this attachment style tend to fixate on whether their partner loves them as much as they love their partner. It is a constant source of anxiety for them because they can never be adequately reassured.

Every small sign that could possibly be interpreted as negative is unequivocally negative to them and causes them significant mental anguish. They tend to measure this on a daily basis, which causes undue stress.

At the heart of it, people with this attachment style are very insecure and don't regard themselves in a very positive light. They doubt that their partner is able to love them as much as they want and deserve. There is an inferiority complex at work here, and constant validation is required in any and all forms—phone calls, texts, physical contact, attention, eye contact.

Their anxiety goes into remission when they are in close contact with their paramour, so they naturally want more and more.

Interestingly, they focus mainly on the love they are receiving, not the love they are giving to their partner. This is a serious problem because the classic definition of love, of course, is a person giving.

By many accounts, true love is measured by what you give, what you sacrifice, and the emotional value you give to another person. This begs the question—do people with this attachment style feel true love, or is a relationship merely a vehicle to validate their self-worth?

How do they act in relationships?

Just as you think they might. They will be uneasy when their partner is out of their sight or they have lost contact with them for a few hours. They need constant affirmation in all forms—verbal and physical. They can tend to get jealous and possessive because they feel anxious if anything appears to threaten their relationship.

Dismissive-Avoidant Attachment

Dismissive-avoidant people are focused on their independence.

They are afraid that once they get into a relationship, they will become saddled with duties and obligations, and will lose control of their life. They are happy with the fact that they are able to make choices in the first place, and are fierce about protecting that privilege. They conflate deep levels of emotional intimacy with a loss of independence and control.

To that effect, they don't feel the need for close emotional relationships because they appear to do more bad than good for them. They characterize themselves as islands or lone wolves by choice.

Their very predictable response is to minimize closeness. They come up with arrangements to keep people at arm's length. It is not uncommon for dismissive-avoidant people to set ground rules that prevent the relationship from truly maturing.

They may accept sexual or physical intimacy, but avoidant people take great pains to minimize true emotional closeness. Unsurprisingly, they can be seen as cold or callous sometimes.

It is not because they do not love the other person. They are afraid that love will rob them of their independence, so they choose different priorities. They don't lack empathy; they just don't let it dictate their actions.

People with this style of attachment sometimes suppress their emotions because of how independent they characterize themselves.

How do they act in relationships?

They have a very doubtful view of relationships, so it's unclear if you'd be able to get them into one. They have a strong fight-or-flight response—meaning that if things don't go their way, they will often prioritize themselves first and leave the relationship.

They can be very difficult to deal with for other attachment styles because their style of attachment is to *not* have attachments. When someone wants to remain by themselves, it can be a waste of time trying to introduce your needs to them. They are stubborn and unwilling to compromise for others because that represents exactly what they hate in relationships.

Ideally, they would be in a relationship with another dismissive-avoidant person, and they would coexist peacefully within their own spaces. Be careful of encroaching on this person's space and forcing them into something.

Fearful-Avoidant Attachment

At first glance, this attachment style appears similar to the dismissive-avoidant.

But the dismissive-avoidant is motivated by very different things. They want to avoid emotional attachment because they feel attachments weaken them; it's a waste of time. Fearful-avoidant people avoid emotional attachment because they feel attachment only leads to heartbreak, disappointment, and feelings of abandonment. Recall that these attachment styles often have their roots in childhood, so people with this attachment style may have experienced childhood traumas or abuse; they may have been abandoned or betrayed by someone they wanted or needed to depend on.

Despite wanting intimate relationships and emotional connections, they have issues opening up and truly getting close to others because a defensive wall shoots up that has been necessary in the past. Vulnerability has hurt them before, and they want to prevent that now and in the future.

They do not have a positive view of others, and have trouble seeing others as particularly trustworthy. Even if you have no history of wrongdoing and say all the right things, you will be constantly scrutinized by people with this attachment style. They are masters of preemptively rejecting others before they have the possibility of being hurt by them.

Because they want to protect themselves at all costs, they are uncomfortable displaying affection, verbal or otherwise. They suppress any positive feelings to keep themselves within the moat of their castle.

How do they act in relationships?

It's hard to get them into one. And when you manage to, they will have trouble committing or opening up. It may take months or years to win their trust, something they don't give easily.

Constant affirmation and validation is necessary. Be careful not to show any signs of doubt or ambiguity, because they might take that as the first sign they should bolt to protect themselves.

Different attachment types produce different relationships, and some attachment types are absolutely toxic when paired with others.

Take another moment to truly see what style you fit into. If you fit into multiple, that's normal as well—but there is always going to be one dominant attachment style that characterizes you. Think about how your views toward attaching to others can drastically change how you act toward them. It might uncover subconscious biases or instances of self-sabotage to ease the discomfort associated with your attachment style.

For example, if you have a dismissive-avoidant person and an anxious-preoccupied person dating, what do you suppose will happen?

From the dismissive-avoidant person's perspective, they want to limit the amount of contact they have and maintain a very independent social life. They view their partner as a small sliver of their life and don't want to commit to obligations that would restrict them.

From the anxious-preoccupied person's perspective, the more points of contact the better. They can never be sure the other person still loves them, so they need to see them as much as possible to ensure they do. They seek commitment, but even a strong and explicit commitment won't stop their anxiety and constant need for validation.

It's not a match made in heaven. Uncovering your attachment style prevents a relationship built on misunderstandings. There's nothing we can do to change our circumstances in the past or our birth order. Unfortunately, they can have wide-ranging consequences on the people we grow into. But as always, nature doesn't have sole control of your personality.

Making Sense of your Past with the Karpman Drama Triangle

Our unique family upbringing can offer us a lot of useful information about ourselves, if only we look with curiosity and open-mindedness. Birth order and attachment style can definitely tell us something about our individual responses to our early life experiences. But there are other theories that allow us to gain a sense of the roles we play in the bigger familial picture.

Canadian psychiatrist Eric Berne proposed a theory he called Transactional Analysis, which shifted the focus from individual personality and characteristics and looked at people in terms of the behavioral relationships existing between them. While more traditional psychoanalytic theory, as well as the work of Adler, focused on personality as a fixed, isolated phenomenon, Berne understood it as a function of social interactions, or "transactions."

You probably understand this concept if you've ever felt that, when returning home to stay with family you don't usually see, you instantly feel as though you are six years old again. Even if you're a successful Type A businessman in ordinary life, when back at home, you seem to slip into all the old roles you played with your parents and siblings. If we want to gain a deeper understanding into who we are and who might like to be, we can take this point of departure. What role did we play in our family of origin?

Berne called these interactions "games." An example game is called "Yes But." The rules go like this: one person recounts their problem at length, and the other person offers solutions. The first person listens but says "yes but" and then gives a list of reasons why that solution could never work. The other person suggests another solution, and round and round they go. Rather than this being a question of either person's personality, it's more about the mutual roles they adopt when together, the games they play, and the rules of that game.

In this same spirit, the Karpman triangle was proposed as a model to analyze the three main positions people can take in any social interaction, in particular "drama." The triangle is a simple map of three positions: the victim, the prosecutor, and the rescuer, in dynamic tension with one another. The connections between each of these roles are based on power and responsibility, and how it flows between actors. If these three elements or actors are present, then drama unfolds. If we understand these roles clearly, we better understand the script as it plays out.

Importantly, just because somebody is playing the role of a victim in a certain drama, it doesn't mean they are permanently a victim. Many games see frequent role reversals, and some may play persecutor in one context and victim in another. What's important to understand with the Karpman triangle is the value of the roles relative to one another—there cannot be a victim without a persecutor, for example.

The victim feels very sorry for themselves. They see themselves as lacking both power and responsibility. Their experience in the situation is one of powerlessness, hopelessness, even shame. Theirs is a passive position, as they feel unable to act. They might feel weak and not entitled to solve problems directly, or make changes. In a strange way, the victim needs the persecutor to validate these feelings.

The persecutor has plenty of power but little sense of responsibility, i.e. they take to blaming others, hurling insults, getting angry, acting superior or authoritarian, or trying to force or control the situation. While the victim's motto is "Poor me!", the persecutor seems to say, "You're wrong and bad!" Persecutors need victims to oppress. They cannot feel righteous or indignant unless there is someone *else* to target and harm as the cause of the trouble, or the one deserving scorn.

The rescuer has both power and a sense of responsibility. They look at the dynamic between persecutor and victim and feel compelled to rush in and save the wronged party. They can also find themselves acting as enablers, getting embroiled in other people's dramas so they can conveniently ignore their own issues. They like to feel needed and in the right. Their position seems to communicate, "I'll help you," and this person may derive a lot of meaning and sense of identity from being compassionate and caring. The truth is, however, that often the rescuer's interest in defending the victim is actually nothing more than avoidance of their own problems, and a bid to appear powerful and needed.

Drama begins when one person takes on the role of persecutor or victim, then draws the corresponding role to them, or pushes someone else into that role. Once the rescuer arrives (they are often explicitly enlisted into the situation), the drama is in full swing. From here, the same dynamic may play over and over again, or the roles may switch in predictable ways.

For example, a father may routinely start a fight with a mother, who then unconsciously enlists her children as rescuers, who then denounce their father's bullying. But then, another drama triangle is set up and the father makes himself a victim by protesting the fact that he is sorry and yet nobody will forgive him. Then the mother switches to the rescuer herself and saves her husband from her children's persecution.

Of course, calling it "drama" may hide the fact that these dynamics can play out in routine, subtle ways every day. You don't have to have come from an unhappy home to have experienced the patterns in the Karpman triangle.

Can you think of common family dramas that unfolded in your early life? Perhaps one person was most often the victim (maybe you?) and another always found themselves the persecutor. Perhaps, in your family, you were always the one who had to come to someone else's rescue.

The point in examining these dynamics is to see if these early experiences may have left residues in your present-day personality. If you always felt like a victim growing up, it's understandable that you would carry some of this hopelessness and passiveness into your adult life. You might be unconsciously always waiting around for the next rescuer to come along and confirm that you have faced an injustice, but that they were going to help you.

Even if you don't neatly identify with any of these three roles, can you think of the role you played at home more generally? Maybe you were always the family nurse, or the disciplinarian. Maybe you were the pride and joy, or the black sheep, or the family clown who was always cheering people up. Maybe you were a protector and provider, or a manager, or a cheerleader—or a mix of all of these! Thinking about the roles you took early on can tell you a lot about the roles you may play in the present.

When thinking about your own early family foundation, it's worth considering *why* these dynamics exist in the first place. Participants in these games get something out of it. They get their (unconscious) needs met through playing that role, without really becoming conscious of their part in the bigger picture. The persecutor, for example, can forever see the bad things in their own life as the fault of someone else. So long as they attack and blame the "bad guy," they never have to take responsibility for their own faults, or make difficult changes to their life.

For Berne, the thing about roles and games was that they were not authentic. They were conditioned, selfish, and superficial responses and not genuine reactions to those around us. We assume the roles we do because, in one way or another, it serves us. This is important: the rescuer is not really acting altruistically, but to satisfy their own needs. Similarly, the victim may or may not be genuinely in the right, only it serves their interests to believe they are.

We can see again the distinction between false self and real self. Our false self might live entirely in this superficial realm where we play out roles rather than express our needs directly and honestly. As an example, consider someone who is feeling afraid of new life challenges and unconfident in their ability to manage them. Without even being consciously aware of it, they may act the victim so they can attract to them someone who will take over, solve their problems, and care for them. This is quite a different story from a mature, self-aware person who owns their own fear and vulnerability, and can communicate to others, "I'm feeling unsure of myself and scared right now." A person who can do this has a far greater self-knowledge than the person who is using games and roles to unconsciously meet their needs.

Codependent dynamics can also be understood in terms of a dance between rescuer and victim. The rescuer, for the satisfaction of their own ego, needs to think of themselves as a savior, and the victim, for the same reason, needs someone to reinforce their image of themselves as powerless. When two people with corresponding needs meet in this way, the bond can be strong and lasting. This is because, unconsciously, neither really wants to abandon their roles. The rescuer doesn't really want to solve the problem, because then they wouldn't be needed anymore, and the victim doesn't really want to be helped, because from then on they would have to take responsibility for themselves.

You might have witnessed many couples who have this eternal dynamic: one pretends to help, the other pretends to always need that help, but nothing ever really changes or improves. They foster dependence with each other. If you happen to be a third person in this dynamic, you might constantly find yourself being drawn in as the bad guy (the persecutor) who is needed to keep the game going. The rescuer keeps the victim depending on them by pretending to solve their problem while in reality enforcing their victimhood. If you had this dynamic at home, either in yourself or in others, there's no doubt it would have affected your sense of self, and how you behaved in *all* social interactions.

A turbulent family past is often best understood as a web of connections, rather than a group of individuals. If each family is a finely balanced ecosystem, what was your role? What were the unspoken rules governing your play in that game? And can you see how this early conditioning remains in your current life?

Whether you agree with Eric Berne or with the Karpman triangle or not, the important part here is that although we are individuals, we have been raised inside complex family systems that have characteristics of their own. You had your own place in that system, and were affected by it just as you affected it.

As an example, think of a woman raised in a home where her stay-at-home mother frequently took on the victim role. This mother might have felt robbed by fate, and behaved as though she were just a timid slave in her marriage to a man she saw as more powerful and important than her. To "save" her mother, the daughter constantly found herself stepping in to make decisions and take action when her mother felt scared or unable. Unconsciously, the daughter began to parent her own mother, becoming protective over her.

When this daughter grows up, she finds she has difficulty dating. She is attracted to strong, capable, and even domineering men (a little like her father), but in the end, she ends up "mothering" them, because of her habit of playing the rescuer. Unwilling to date a self-righteous martyr, boyfriends come and go, and the daughter feels conflicted—until she realizes that if she wants a mature relationship, she needs to stop acting like it's her job to take care of everyone.

Here we see something important: just because something is ingrained in us from childhood, and even if some aspect of ourselves really is part of our personality, it doesn't mean we can't consciously make the decision to take on a different, healthier role for ourselves. When we consciously look at the part we have played in life, we give ourselves the chance to stop and decide to play another part.

Takeaways:

- An interesting subset of personality science is the ways people theorize we are influenced by our upbringings. Since this is largely while we were young children, this is said to be mostly unconscious and instinctual according to our early experiences.

- One theory is Adler's birth order theory, which states that the interaction between the first, middle, and youngest children in a family and how they compete for the affection and attention of the parents create personality traits by themselves.
- According to this theory, the firstborn receives all their parents' love and affection until the second child comes long. This results in the first child being "dethroned," and they might react either positively or engage in bad behaviors to win their parents' attention back. Generally, the firstborn becomes bossy, tries to dominate the other children, and might be more predisposed toward leadership. The second child is the "peacemaker" and is more cooperative but can become rebellious once the third child comes along.
- The third child, who is least likely to be dethroned, receives the most attention from their parents. As such, they become attention-seekers, dependent on others,

and selfish because they haven't been told no by their parents often enough.

- The other prevailing theory on unconscious upbringings is attachment theory by Bowlby, which states that the way we view relationships with others is a direct result of how safe and secure we feel in regard to our caretakers as children. If you felt secure, you likely have secure attachments as an adult. If you felt less than secure, you could have any of the other three types of attachments: anxious-preoccupied, dismissive-avoidant, fearful-avoidant.

- A third theory is the Karpman drama triangle. According to this, all of us take up one of three roles in any interaction: the victim, the prosecutor, and the rescuer. As the names suggest, victims generally feel sorry for themselves, while prosecutors love questioning the victim and blaming them for their problems. The rescuer swoops in to interject and mediate whenever necessary. The role you occupied in your past experiences and interactions with

friends and family can tell you a lot
about yourself in the present.

Chapter 6. Myers, Briggs, and Keirsey

We'll end our book on one final personality theory that has become popular in recent years. Many people take tests in the hope of achieving a certain result. Especially with the tests that follow, many mistakenly assume that one type is better than another, or are secretly proud that they have scored as one of the rarer types. But as you read on, bear in mind that doing personality tests is a way to **discover what you already are**.

It's tempting to get very attached to the concept of this or that personality type, but it's worth remembering that these subtypes are generalizations, and they are necessarily simplified—at the end of the day, we are all individuals! These tests can be a great *starting point* for your journey into self-discovery, but they are certainly not the end point. If you disagree with an outcome, that's completely fine. You are not trying to fit yourself to the test. What's important is that these tests are used as tools to help you gain a deeper and more genuine understanding of who you are.

There are a lot of different personality tests out there. This chapter will explore the Myers-Briggs Type Indicator (MBTI) as well as the subsequent Keirsey Temperaments. These temperaments were a result of the MBTI to help organize it better and create more relatable classifications and categories.

The MBTI has also been one of the most popular ones for people to use when conceiving of personality. It's highly doubtful that people haven't heard of this test, as many have taken various forms of it without even knowing. Overall, the test is based on four very distinct *dichotomies*, which you can imagine as simply being traits. People have compared the MBTI as one that purely functions as a modern horoscope. The thing to remember, though, is that this doesn't mean it's no longer beneficial.

The MBTI was developed around the time of World War II. Myers and Briggs were two housewives and observed many people taking job opportunities. However, it bothered them that many of those people were taking jobs that didn't necessarily pertain to their skills.

These two were also very interested in the theories and works of Carl Jung, a Swiss psychiatrist. Jung believed that archetypes came from models of people, behavior, and their personalities. He strongly suggested that these archetypes came innately due to the influence of human behavior. Overall, he concluded that people inherit these archetypes in the same manner that they inherit instinctive patterns of behavior.

Because of Jung's theories and influence, the MBTI was developed. Myers and Briggs's intention was to produce a useful enough test that geared specifically toward women heading into the workforce. The goal was to give them this test to help them find job assignments that were most suitable and aligned with their personalities.

The MBTI and Personality Types

Carl Jung theorized that people and their psychological types could be characterized by general traits along three spectrums.

For personality, the spectrum has at two ends: extroverted (E) versus introverted (I).

For perception, the spectrum has at two ends: sensing (S) versus intuition (N).

Then, for judging, the spectrum has at two ends: thinking (T) versus feeling (F).

These three areas of preferences were introduced as dichotomies by Jung. These dichotomies were considered to be bipolar dimensions where each of the poles represented different preferences. Utilizing this proposal by Jung, Myers suggested that the judging-perceiving relationship was the fourth dichotomy for influential personality types—judging (J) versus perceiving (P).

The idea is that everyone can measure themselves along these four spectrums, and certain patterns will emerge so that you are able to discover your personality type.

The first criterion, extroversion versus introversion, signifies the source as well as the direction of a person's energy expression.

An extrovert and his energy expression mainly happens in the external world. When in the presence and company of others, extroverts are able to recharge. For an introvert, his source of energy mainly happens in his internal world. Having space to himself is ideal and can prove to be the best mode of recharging that energy expression.

Extroverted people are action-oriented in comparison to introverted people, who are more thought-oriented. In a classroom, extroverted students like to participate in group discussions and presentations. Their interactions with other students provide that sense of charge for their personality types. An introverted student would rather work alone on projects and feels somewhat uncomfortable during whole class discussions. They like being able to think on their own and work through assessments by themselves as well.

The second criterion, sensing versus intuition, represents how someone perceives information.

When a person is sensing, he or she believes information received directly from that external world. This may come in the form of using his or her five senses—sight, smell, touch, taste, and hearing. Decisions come in more immediate and practical ways.

For someone using intuition, he or she believes information from an internal world—their intuition—over external evidence. This comes in the form of having that "gut feeling." He or she digs a little deeper into detail and tries to connect patterns. It may take a little longer before a decision can be made.

Sensing has to do with believing information that is more concrete and tangible over intuition, which is more about looking at the underlying theories or principles that may come out of data. A police officer will always use evidence and data to support their claims for making an arrest because this information is measurable. On the other side, a lawyer would exhibit more intuition because there could be a lot more to the context being presented, which helps him defend his clients.

The third criterion, thinking versus feeling, has to do with how a person processes information. Thinking is when someone makes a decision mainly through the process of logical thinking. They also think in tangible means, where they look to rules to guide their decision-making.

Opposite to this is the feeling where someone would rather make a decision based on emotion. For decisions, these people look to what they value as a means for choosing their best option. They may deem thinkers as being cold and heartless.

Thinking mostly occurs when someone lays out all the possible and practical reasons for making a sound decision. Basically, someone is going to make a decision using one's brain. Feeling is when someone will make that decision from the heart. People who purchase homes will either sign the paperwork based on pricing and resale value (thinking) versus those buying to stay in their old neighborhood (feeling).

The fourth criterion, judging versus perceiving, is how someone will implement the information he has processed.

Organizing life events is how someone would judge and later use it, as a rule, to stick to the plan. These people like to have order and structure. Their sense of self-control comes from being able to control their environments as much as possible. Judging types will normally use previous experiences as a catalyst to either continue or avoid certain behaviors later. They also like to see things settled and done with.

Improvisation and option exploration is what someone would do with perceiving. These people like having options and see organization being a limit to their potential. They like to make choices when they are necessary, and like to explore problem-solving and strategizing. Perceiving types will somewhat live in the moment and understand that there are multitudes of options available to them, regardless of how other experiences have occurred in the past.

There are a total of sixteen different combinations, or personality types, that can come out of the permutations of preferences in the mentioned four dichotomies. These help to represent one of the two poles that each person can have in terms of a dominant dichotomy. So this is what defines the sixteen different personality types, as each can be assigned a four-letter acronym. These are the corresponding combinations:

Sixteen Personality Types

ISTJ	ISTP	INTP	ESTP
introverted sensor thinker judger	introverted sensor thinker perceiver	introverted intuitor thinker perceiver	Extroverted sensor thinker perceiver
ISFP	ISFJ	INTJ	ESTJ
introverted sensor feeler perceiver	introverted sensor feeler judger	introverted intuitor thinker judger	Extroverted sensor thinker judger
INFP	INFJ	ESFP	ENFP
introverted intuitor feeler perceiver	introverted intuitor feeler judger	Extroverted sensor feeler perceiver	Extroverted intuitor feeler perceiver
ESFJ	ENTP	ENTJ	ENFJ
Extroverted sensor feeler judger	Extroverted intuitor thinker perceiver	Extroverted intuitor thinker judger	Extroverted intuitor feeler judger

When analyzing this chart, one could utilize the following rules:

The first letter corresponds to the first letter preference of general attitude.
E: extroversion or I: introversion

The second letter corresponds to the preference within the dimension of sensing-intuition.

S: sensing or N: intuition

The third letter corresponds to the preference within the pair of thinking-feeling.
T: thinking or F: feeling

The fourth letter corresponds to the preference within the pair of judging-perceiving.
J: judging or P: perception

So for instance, ISTP would stand for introverted, sensing, thinking, and perceiving. These individuals might be those daredevils always looking for their next adventure and contemplating this over a bottle of their favorite recreational beverage.

ESFJ would stand for extroverted, sensing, feeling, and judging. These people might be those you see on television sitcoms who gossip about everyone and whose main goal in life is to be married with kids, only to be able to gossip with other moms around the neighborhood.

The point scores on each can also vary from person to person, even those considered to be the same personality type. This shares similarities with the Big Five personality traits, and functions in the same vein of applying specific traits to people.

Shortcomings of the MBTI

Although the test provides insight into one personality, it does have some shortcomings that make it difficult to rely on all of its data.

For one, the sixteen types described are only stereotypes. This means that they don't necessarily describe the individuals. Stereotypes, in their own way, are not the ideal ways to judge anyone. They never represent an entire population, so it becomes a slippery slope when trying to use it in categorizing others.

Another shortcoming is that the descriptions for each only appear to be accurate because of the Forer effect, also known as the Barnum effect (1956). The Barnum effect is where people have a tendency to conform to generalized statements if they are supposedly about them—people will look for what they are told and what they want, even if it is barely there. Fortune tellers and astrologers use this method to prove to their customers that they have this "paranormal gift."

People who like to use their horoscopes as ways of leading their lives are perfect examples of those who utilize the Barnum effect. They read through the descriptions for each day, study the behaviors of their own signs, and, in a sense, create a reality for themselves and believe it has to do with what they've read and studied.

Although this is naturally a human trait, it doesn't help to explain the typology or results of the MBTI test. This is because the Barnum effect was based purely off people's responses alone.

Another shortcoming is that the MBTI only gives answers that are definitive, and it doesn't account for the fact that people are usually not one-sided on their traits. People aren't entirely on one end of the spectrum over another. The MBTI only gives people two ends of the spectrum, not anything in between. Thus, most people can be moderate in many other traits.

For instance, you might be forty-five percent extroverted and fifty-five percent introverted, but the MBTI would call you an introvert without subtlety.

Lastly, the MBTI's reliability is poor because it claims that each personality type is inborn and remains with people throughout their lives. A researcher, David Pittenger, studies that when a test-retest interval is done over a short amount of time, as many as fifty percent of people will get classified into a different type.

Rightly so, Pittenger also observed that this occurs due to the fact that there are cutoff points driving the dimensions. This issue can be seen by the geographical analogy mentioned—small changes at the boundaries, where most people will be, are able to produce a huge change in the overall result.

Over time and as expected, people can change. Results from their MBTI can change in a span of either days or weeks depending on their moods or influences from their external and internal environments. These factors will say nothing about their actual personality types.

Keirsey's Temperaments Sorter

One of the other popular ways of understanding the MBTI is through David Keirsey's four temperaments. He helped to organize the information people received from MBTI to narrow it down from sixteen personality types to four general temperaments instead. Within each temperament, Keirsey also identified two types of roles one might play instinctively and naturally.

The Four Temperaments

"The Guardian"
This happens when someone results in being a sensor and judger. These people have a longing to belong, contribute to their society, and are confident in their own abilities.

Guardians are also concrete and more organized. They seek security and belonging while still being concerned with responsibilities and duties. Logistics is one of their greatest strengths; they are excellent at organization, facilitation, supporting, and checking. Their two roles are administrators and conservators.

Administrators tend to be the proactive and directive versions of guardians. They are most efficient in regulating, and their attentive inspectors and supervisors are their highest role variants. Conservators are the reactive and expressive versions of guardians, and their best intelligence is supporting.

"The Artisan"

This occurs when an individual tests as being a sensor and perceiver. These individuals live freely and through a lot of action-filled events.

Artisans are completely adaptable. They usually seek out stimulation and virtuosity. Artisans are highly concerned with making a large impact, and one of their greatest strengths happens to be tactics. They are extremely proficient in troubleshooting, problem-solving, and agility. They also have the ability to manipulate tools, instruments, and equipment.

Artisans have two roles—operators and entertainers. Operators are the directive and proactive version of artisans. They have a high capacity to expedite, and are the attentive crafters and promoters of the role variants. Entertainers are the more informative and reactive versions of artisans. They have a great way of improvising and are attentive to details.

Keirsey estimates that about eighty percent of the population is categorized as being artisans or guardians.

"The Idealist"
This happens when someone results in being an intuitive and feeler. These people find meaning in their lives while helping themselves and others be the best versions of themselves. They value uniqueness and individuality.

Idealists are abstract and can be compassionate. They work to seek significance and meaning in almost everything. They are concerned with their own personal growth and being able to find their true identities. They are very good at diplomacy and have strengths in clarifying, unifying, individualizing, and inspiring others. They have two roles—mentors and advocates.

Mentors are the proactive and directive versions of idealists. They are very good at developing, and their attentive variant roles are counselors and teachers. Advocates are the reactive and informative idealists who are very good at mediating.

"The Rational"
This occurs when someone tests as being an intuitive and thinker. There is always a drive to increase these people's knowledge, and they are highly competent. They usually have a sense of personal satisfaction.

Rationals are objective and abstract. They seek to be masters of their craft and have self-control. They are usually concerned with their own type of knowledge and competence. Strategy is their greatest strength, and they have the ability to logically investigate, engineer, conceptualize, theorize, and coordinate. Their two roles are coordinators and engineers.

Coordinators are the proactive and directive versions of rationals. They are great at arranging, and their variant roles are masterminds and field marshals. Engineers are the reactive and informative versions of rationals.

Like the MBTI, Keirsey's temperament sorter has the ability to determine personality type based on four elements in people—energy or stimulant to a person, how people process information, make decisions, and tend to live their lives. Both tests allow a person to rate themselves based on a series of statements.

But they also differ when it comes to interpretation. Keirsey's assessment looks at the relation between each personality characteristic versus the MBTI focusing on each one individually. Keirsey personalities are also grouped by how people see the world, while the MBTI prioritizes how people relate to other people. The MBTI might be a more accurate account because how people relate to others is much more intimate and reliable than how they see the world, which can be full of stereotypical factors.

When it comes to the four different temperaments, Keirsey and MBTI have specific ways of analyzing the data for people's personality traits.

First, how people interact with others will look different between the MBTI and Keirsey tests. Extroverted people would prefer to spend time collaborating with others and sharing ideas through MBTI's interpretation. Keirsey would describe these people as being expressive and energized when they're in contact with others.

MBTI would describe introverted people as those preferring to spend time alone, drawing on their own thoughts. Keirsey would say that these people are reserved and find energy in being alone. They do like to socialize but in more intimate settings.

Second, take how people process information and the world around them as an example, here.

MBTI would interpret a sensing person to prefer their reliance on senses when gathering and evaluating information.

Keirsey's interpretation of this same individual would be that he or she is an observer and pays more attention to the outside world. He or she would seek out facts to make an overall judgment.

For intuition, MBTI would say that these people rely on their instincts by using abstract thinking, whereas Keirsey would say that these people enjoy introspection and daydreaming. Sometimes, they'll end up missing a lot of what's going on around them.

An example would be the difference between a journalist for a newspaper and a blog writer on a personal webpage.

Third, when it comes to governing decision-making, MBTI would say that thinking people prefer to make decisions carefully, weighing all of their options prior to doing so. On the Keirsey assessment, these people would drive their decisions by logic and hide their emotions because they may be embarrassed by intense feelings that could potentially go out of control.

When it comes to feeling, MBTI would say these people prefer to make decisions instantly through their emotions. Keirsey interprets these people as valuing the importance of feelings over logic and following their hearts.

And for the fourth, when it comes to organizing their lives, MBTI would indicate that judgment people would prefer to have control in their surroundings so they can anticipate what comes next. Keirsey would describe these people as being schedulers and having a strong desire for structure.

People who score perception on the Myers-Briggs test would like the flexibility to explore all of their options in order to learn from them. Keirsey would interpret these same people as probers who are less likely to tie themselves down to a schedule since they are so open to alternative options. An instance of this would be the difference between a highly organized event planner and a traveling musician.

Keirsey's temperament sorter has the ability to take personality trait assessment a few steps deeper than that of MBTI. It helps to evaluate a person's results as it relates to other traits, while MBTI focuses on each trait individually. But like MBTI, no individual can ever be just one temperament. Almost every single person will have traits in all temperaments, so it would be extremely difficult to pinpoint just one category.

Temperaments overall have the ability to give people a better sense into how they are and what they can do to change their personalities. Being a personality type merely tells someone how they are, but temperaments look beyond that surface-level interpretation. Temperament identification allows people to score themselves and potentially make a change for the better. They have more self-awareness about themselves and can better adapt if needed.

Both tests have the ability to test people's personalities, but careful considerations should be made when evaluating the results. Each test will yield particular results that have more priority over another. In the end, nothing definitive may have been discovered except a helpful template to guide your life decisions.

Takeaways:

- The MBTI, though helpful as a guideline, can sometimes suffer from people treating it like a horoscope and reading into their type what they wish to see about themselves. However, from a theoretical perspective, its been framed considering Jungian insights into the human personality.
- The MBTI functions on four distinct traits and how much of each trait you are or are not. The traits are generally introverted/extroverted (your general attitude toward others), intuitive/feeling (how you perceive information), thinking/feeling (how you process information), and perceiving/judging (how you implement

information). Thus, this creates sixteen distinct personality types.

- The MBTI does suffer from some shortcomings, including the lack of subtlety when most people are a bit of each trait, the usage of stereotyping to classify people, and the lack of consistency when people score differently depending on their current moods and circumstances. It also encourages the Barnum effect wherein generalized statements relating to you seem truer than they actually are. This is why they've been compared to horoscopes.
- The Keirsey temperaments were a way of organizing the same information gleaned from the MBTI. Here, there are four distinct temperaments, each with two types of roles, instead of sixteen personality types. The four temperaments are guardian, artisan, idealistic, and rational. Keirsey himself estimated that up to eighty percent of the population fall into the first two temperaments. The guardian is generally very organized and lives a

structured life, while artisans require constant stimulation. The latter are also highly adaptable.

- The MBTI and Keirsey temperaments are similar in that both rely on certain stereotypes to convey personality-related attributes. They also use similar metrics for these stereotypes. However, the difference lies in the way both frameworks analyze the four distinct traits listed earlier. While the MBTI focuses on each trait individually, the Kiersey temperaments analyze them in relation to each other. Overall, take the results from both tests with a pinch of salt.

Summary Guide

<u>**CHAPTER 1: FINDING YOUR VALUES**</u>

- A value is a rule, principle, or belief that gives meaning to your life. It is usually something you consider very important in life and base many of your decisions around. This is why when you're confused about what to do in a certain situation or circumstances that you find yourself in, the cause is usually a lack of clarity on what your real values are.
- If you're not sure what your values are in life, don't worry; discovering them is not hard. However, the process does take time, and you won't simply wake up tomorrow with complete knowledge of what your values are.
- The first step to discovering what your values are is to simply abandon all preconceived notions you have of who you are. Often, the values we have been

living by are actually derived externally. This can be through our family, culture, historical era, etc. By starting from a clean slate, we avoid such influences from clouding our judgment regarding our true values.

- Next, think about the things that you feel most strongly about. This could be personal success, close family bonds, serving others in the form of social work, etc. Finding one will often lead you to other values you hold because they point to a "higher" value you possess. Thus, valuing family over career means that your interpersonal relationships in general are valuable to you.

- Once you have a complete list of values, think about your goals in life and how your values align with them. Are the things you're doing now in conjunction with your values and goals? If not, think of ways you can change that and live a life that is truer to your real self.

- As you discover your values, doing actions that promote them will help you decide what it is that you really consider important.

CHAPTER 2. THE BIG FIVE PERSONALITY TRAITS

- The Big Five personality traits are one of the first attempts to classify people based on specific traits rather than as a whole. You can remember the traits easily with the acronym OCEAN: openness to experience (trying new things), conscientiousness (being cautious and careful), extroversion (drawing energy from others and social situations), agreeableness (warm and sympathetic), and neuroticism (anxious and high-strung).

- Each attribute in the OCEAN acronym has some advantages and disadvantages. For example, being neurotic makes you highly prone to stress and anxiety, but it also leads you to realistically evaluate situations and problems better. Being agreeable generally ensures that you are well-liked, but it means you might be less successful professionally.

- Extroverts generally experience more positive experiences and are renowned for being the life of the party. However, they can also be exhausting to be around, especially for introverts. Being conscientious makes it very easy to pursue and fulfil your goals, have a structured routine, and acquire higher social status. But if you're too high on this trait, it might also make you boring and dull because you aren't spontaneous enough. Lastly, openness to experience means that you're constantly experiencing new and exciting things in your life. However, it also makes it easy for you to struggle with routine since you need higher levels of stimulation to remain interested in what you're doing.

- Unlike other assessments in this book, there have actually been determined to be a winning formula for these traits—not per se, but if you display certain traits, you are more likely to have better mental health and increased happiness. If you are more of the first four traits (OCEA) and less neurotic, you will tend to be happier and more fulfilled in life. It's not hard to understand why—you'll have more experiences, you'll live longer from your caution, you'll have a wider social circle and support system, you'll get along better with others, and you'll be less anxious and more relaxed.

CHAPTER 3. THE STORIES WE CREATE

- The narratives and stories we tell ourselves about who we are constitute a large part of our sense of self. However, few of us have actually taken the time to sit down and think about the stories we tell ourselves about our achievements, who we are, what we're good at, etc. By reconfiguring and identifying our stories that are grounded in past experiences we've had, we can construct a more coherent identity for ourselves and discover who we really are.
- Sometimes the best way to discover something about ourselves is to ask seemingly innocent questions, then read between the lines. The way we answer these types of questions can be more honest and indicative than intentionally trying to figure out your personality and identity.
- The first way to do this is through the

seven stories exercise, which implores you to first note down twenty-five of your most highly coveted achievements. Then, you must narrow it down to get your seven greatest accomplishments and write the stories involved in those triumphs. Try to recall as much detail as you can, and then analyze what these stories really tell you about yourself. Finally, write down two hundred possible ways you can use the results of your analysis to express your values and identity better in the world around you. What comes out in the story will tell you more about who you are and what you seek than trying to answer those questions alone.

- The second method to discover yourself is through Carl Jung's personality test, which consists of four steps: name a color, name an animal, name a body of water, and think about a white room. The ensuing adjectives you use to describe each of those answers will tell you something specific about your personality that your psyche may not consciously have realized.

CHAPTER 4. SELF-AWARENESS QUESTIONS

- Self-awareness is important, but not easily gained. That's why it's so highly valued. Methods like using personality tests and engaging with certain exercises have been taken up in previous chapters. This one is about asking yourself particular questions, the answers to which will reveal major components of who you are and what you truly value in life.

- The best way to gain self-awareness is to ask about your behaviors and actions, not your intentions or thoughts. Your thoughts are too easily corrupted or otherwise simply not representative of what you actually feel. When you can analyze your behaviors and actions, you can then glean real information about yourself.

- There are several questions you can ask yourself. For example, what is one achievement that you're most proud of and one thing you've done that you're most ashamed of? The achievement you're proud of will reveal a lot about what you value, and what kind of skills you are good at that made the achievement possible in the first place. On the other hand, the thing you're ashamed of is something you should be wary about repeating and reminding yourself that you do not want to be the same person who did that horrible thing.

- Another great question is to ask yourself what feels effortless, and what is always exhausting to do. Everyone has something that they're naturally very good at. Discovering what this is in your case can take some trial and error, but the time investment will be worth it. Similarly, the thing you find exhausting is probably not a large part of what you value.

- A third question, among others, is what you would do if you only had one month left to live. Say you've been diagnosed with cancer—what are the things you would stop doing immediately, and what would you do more often with the little time you have left?

- These questions are all vague and have

no right answer, but one can immediately see why they're insightful and reveal things about ourselves that we may not have thought about.

CHAPTER 5. UNCONSCIOUS UPBRINGINGS

- An interesting subset of personality science is the ways people theorize we are influenced by our upbringings. Since this is largely while we were young children, this is said to be mostly unconscious and instinctual according to our early experiences.
- One theory is Adler's birth order theory, which states that the interaction between the first, middle, and youngest children in a family and how they compete for the affection and attention of the parents create personality traits by themselves.
- According to this theory, the firstborn receives all their parents' love and affection until the second child comes long. This results in the first child being "dethroned," and they might react either positively or engage in bad behaviors to

9

win their parents' attention back.
Generally, the firstborn becomes bossy,
tries to dominate the other children, and
might be more predisposed toward
leadership. The second child is the
"peacemaker" and is more cooperative
but can become rebellious once the third
child comes along.

- The third child, who is least likely to be
  dethroned, receives the most attention
  from their parents. As such, they become
  attention-seekers, dependent on others,
  and selfish because they haven't been
  told no by their parents often enough.
- The other prevailing theory on
  unconscious upbringings is attachment
  theory by Bowlby, which states that the
  way we view relationships with others is
  a direct result of how safe and secure we
  feel in regard to our caretakers as
  children. If you felt secure, you likely
  have secure attachments as an adult. If
  you felt less than secure, you could have
  any of the other three types of
  attachments: anxious-preoccupied,
  dismissive-avoidant, fearful-avoidant.

- A third theory is the Karpman drama triangle. According to this, all of us take up one of three roles in any interaction: the victim, the prosecutor, and the rescuer. As the names suggest, victims generally feel sorry for themselves, while prosecutors love questioning the victim and blaming them for their problems. The rescuer swoops in to interject and mediate whenever necessary. The role you occupied in your past experiences and interactions with friends and family can tell you a lot about yourself in the present.

CHAPTER 6. MYERS, BRIGGS, AND KEIRSEY

- The MBTI, though helpful as a guideline, can sometimes suffer from people treating it like a horoscope and reading into their type what they wish to see about themselves. However, from a theoretical perspective, its been framed considering Jungian insights into the human personality.
- The MBTI functions on four distinct traits and how much of each trait you

are or are not. The traits are generally introverted/extroverted (your general attitude toward others), intuitive/feeling (how you perceive information), thinking/feeling (how you process information), and perceiving/judging (how you implement information). Thus, this creates sixteen distinct personality types.

- The MBTI does suffer from some shortcomings, including the lack of subtlety when most people are a bit of each trait, the usage of stereotyping to classify people, and the lack of consistency when people score differently depending on their current moods and circumstances. It also encourages the Barnum effect wherein generalized statements relating to you seem truer than they actually are. This is why they've been compared to horoscopes.

- The Keirsey temperaments were a way of organizing the same information gleaned from the MBTI. Here, there are four distinct temperaments, each with two types of roles, instead of sixteen personality types. The four temperaments are guardian, artisan, idealistic, and rational. Keirsey himself estimated that up to eighty percent of the population fall into the first two temperaments. The guardian is generally very organized and lives a structured life, while artisans require constant stimulation. The latter are also highly adaptable.

- The MBTI and Keirsey temperaments are similar in that both rely on certain stereotypes to convey personality-related attributes. They also use similar metrics for these stereotypes. However, the difference lies in the way both frameworks analyze the four distinct traits listed earlier. While the MBTI focuses on each trait individually, the Kiersey temperaments analyze them in relation to each other. Overall, take the results from both tests with a pinch of salt.

Printed in Great Britain
by Amazon